THE BOTTOM TRANSLATION

Other Works by Jan Kott in English

Shakespeare Our Contemporary
Theater Notebook 1947–1967
The Eating of the Gods
The Theater of Essence

THE BOTTOM TRANSLATION

Marlowe and Shakespeare and the Carnival Tradition

JAN KOTT

Translated by Daniela Miedzyrzecka and Lillian Vallee

NORTHWESTERN UNIVERSITY PRESS / EVANSTON, ILLINOIS

Published by Northwestern University Press
Evanston, Illinois 60201
Printed in the United States of America

Library of Congress Cataloging-in-Publication Data

Kott, Jan.
 The bottom translation.

 Includes bibliographies and index.
 1. Shakespeare, William, 1564–1616—Criticism and
interpretation. 2. Shakespeare, William, 1564–1616.
Tempest. 3. Shakespeare, William, 1564–1616.
Midsummer night's dream. 4. Marlowe, Christopher,
1564–1593. Doctor Faustus. I. Title.
PR2979.P58K5   1987   822.3′3   87-1719
ISBN 0–8101–0737–6
ISBN 0–8101–0738–4 (pbk.)

"Bless thee, Bottom, bless thee! Thou art translated"
—*A Midsummer Night's Dream*

Acknowledgements

I began to write some chapters of this book almost fifteen years ago, as a Guggenheim Fellow in 1972–73. I completed this book in 1985–86 during the wonderful year I spent as a Getty Scholar at the Getty Center for the History of Art and the Humanities in Santa Monica. I would like to thank the Guggenheim Foundation and the Getty Center for their assistance and generous support.

Many thanks are also due to my editor and friend, Jonathan Brent, who was the most attentive and severe reader of these essays.

The essays collected in *The Bottom Translation* were revised and often expanded from the following original publications and are used here with permission: "The Two Hells of Doctor Faustus: A Polytheatrical Vision" from *New Theatre Quarterly;* "The Bottom Translation" from *Assays;* "The Tempest, or Repetition" from *Mosaic;* "The Aeneid and The Tempest" from *Arion;* "Prospero, or the Director" from *Theater;* "Ran, or the End of the World" from *The New York Review of Books;* "The Cruel Webster" from John Webster, *The White Devil and the Duchess of Malfi*, Longman Study Text (Essex: Longman House, 1986).

Contents

List of Illustrations

SHAKESPEARE'S PUCK,

AND HIS

Folkslore,

ILLUSTRATED FROM

THE SUPERSTITIONS OF ALL NATIONS,

BUT MORE ESPECIALLY FROM THE

EARLIEST RELIGION AND RITES OF NORTHERN EUROPE AND THE WENDS.

BY

WILLIAM BELL, Phil. Dr.

HONORARY MEMBER OF THE HISTORIC SOCIETY FOR LANCASHIRE AND CHESHIRE, AND CORRESPONDING MEMBER OF THE SOCIETY OF ANTIQUARIES FOR NORMANDY, AT CAEN.

P Cruik

LONDON:

PRINTED FOR THE AUTHOR,

17 GOWER PLACE, EUSTON SQUARE,

WHERE APPLICATION IS TO BE MADE.

MDCCCLII,

Ego sum Papa.

The Two Hells of Doctor Faustus:
A Polytheatrical Vision

I

In one of Rembrandt's etchings (probably done between 1651 and 1653), Faust is depicted in his study. In the lower right-hand corner, there is an early Renaissance astrolabe fixed to a wooden ring. Faust wears a wide, loose coat and has a nightcap or white turban on his head, much like those worn by the Jewish elders of Amsterdam in other paintings. It is daybreak, and Faust is gazing at the first rays of sunlight. The rectangular window is made up of smaller panes, as in stained-glass windows finished with soldered arches in older German colleges. Under the window is a radiant illuminated shield, with three circles bearing signs. In the middle circle is Christ's monogram. On the outer circle are the letters AGLA (written in reverse order), the old Hebrew blessing. Frances Yates has speculated that this Faust-sage in the Rembrandt etching, the embodiment of inspired melancholy, is immersed in the mysteries of the Christian Cabala.[1]

On the title page of the 1616 edition of Christopher Marlowe's *The Tragicall History of the Life and Death of Doctor Faustus*, a Magus is shown in his study. A spherical cage with a bird inside, a clock, and a crucifix hang on the wall. Faustus wears a beret and formal gown trimmed in fur. He has a moustache twisted up at the ends and is somewhat chubby. No shade of melancholy is in his face. He holds a rod in his right hand and points it at the circle of tiles bearing magical signs: Arabic and Hebrew letters joined with symbols of the sun, moon, and planets. In his left hand he holds a book from which he reads incantations. In Marlowe's drama, the most evocative line is the last one in the Prologue: "And this the man that in his study sits." Faustus' study is at the University of Wittenberg.

Bakhtin introduces the concept of the chronotope in *Dialogic Imagination*. The joining of time and space in one category, used by Bakhtin in his analyses of the novel, seems to be even more useful for the interpretation of drama. The stage is a perfect image of this blending of time and space. Onstage every time has its particular setting, and within this setting a time is almost a protagonist of the drama.

Perhaps the most revealing aspect of Marlowe's dramaturgy is his choice of setting. In *The Jew of Malta*, the first place of action is a counting-house, where a moneylender inspects his treasury—"Infinite riches in a little room" (1.1.37). To Karl Marx, this scene would have provided an excellent image of "the first era of capitalist accumulation." Barabas sits "in his counting house, with heaps of gold before him": his riches were not notes, checks, or bills but gold coins— "crowns," so called because of the royal stamp depicting a crown.[2]

A chronotope even more revealing than the Renaissance counting-house of the moneylender is the study of the Renaissance magus at Wittenberg University. Before Protestant orthodoxy curtailed the free study of nature and the range of theological and philosophical disputes, Wittenberg was a center of Renaissance art and science dominating all of Germany. If we allow ourselves a certain freedom of chronology, we can situate Hamlet and Faust in Wittenberg during the same time span. This would produce a beautiful literary chronotope. The first "real" Faust, a self-invested conjurer and astrologer, sodomite and globetrotter, was expelled from all the universities, but probably stayed in Wittenberg on more than one occasion. In addition to casting horoscopes, he practiced necromancy and could have told Hamlet, over a glass of sack in a local tavern, how he summoned the ghosts of the dead. Perhaps this is why the Prince of Denmark was not a little incredulous when he saw the ghost of his father walking along the castle platform at midnight. The play *Faust and Hamlet in Wittenberg* is still awaiting its author.

And this the man that in his study sits.

Offstage lie the real world, the university, and the city; then come Germany, France, and Italy; "And from America the golden fleece" (1.2.130); and further, in the now half-mythical geography, "Lapland giants." The globe had been traversed all round. Both Magellan and Columbus were con-temporaries of the first Faust.

Faustus' study, like Prospero's "uninhabited isle," is a new "theater of the world." The *axis mundi* passes through his Wittenberg study; on it lie Heaven and Hell. The heavens invite transgression. Leonardo, Faustus' contemporary, drew models of airships that were flawless in construction and had astounding equilibrium, but the wood and metal which he used were too heavy; human muscles could not lift the wings of this Renaissance Icarus.

> His waxen wings did mount above his reach,
> And melting, heavens conspired his overthrow.
> (Prologue 31–32)

II

In the German *Faustbuch* (its English translation, published in 1592, was the main source for Marlowe's *Faustus*), the pact with Mephistophilis had guaranteed that "the spirit should tell nothing but that which is true." The devil is not allowed to lie. Nor is science. The pact with darkness inspires both fascination and horror. It horrified even Thomas Mann: "Here try the brains to get a deity!" exclaims Marlowe's Faustus in his Wittenberg cell.

Not until Romanticism does Faust demand the gift of eternal youth from the devil. The Renaissance Faust did not prize youth very highly—with power one can have any man and any woman. Even Helen. Eternal youth was not the price Faustus exacted in exchange for his soul. He had other, far more serious ambitions.

> Oh, what a world of profit and delight,
> Of power, of honour, of omnipotence,
> Is promised to the studious artisan!

> All things that move between the quiet poles
> Shall be at my command.
>
> (1.1.53–57)

In no other great Renaissance text is the fascination with hermetic knowledge more apparent than in Pico della Mirandola's *Oration on the Dignity of Man*, written in 1486, when the first German Faust was not much more than five years old.

> . . . magic has two forms, one of which depends entirely on the work and authority of demons, a thing to be abhorred, so help me God of truth, and a monstrous thing: the other, when it is rightly pursued, is nothing else than the utter perfection of natural philosophy . . .[3]

The distinction between the experiments with elements and magical spells was far from clear. Numerical conjurations with the images of little angels and Arabic and Hebrew letters were discovered even in Newton's manuscripts.[4] Hermetic speculation has accompanied astrology for centuries, representing perhaps the prescientific intuition that matter and energy are interrelated in a mathematical formula.

There were two heavens over Doctor Faustus' study: the heaven of astrology and the heaven of astronomy. The planets moved in conjunction with the signs of the zodiac and forecast victory or defeat in battle, happy or disastrous events. Seven movable spheres rotated around the unmoving Earth: the moon, Mercury, Venus, the Sun, Mars, Jupiter, and Saturn. Above them was the firmament, or the "eighth" sphere of fixed stars. But who moved the moving stars? Doctor Faustus of Renaissance Wittenberg no longer believed in the angels, called "dominions" or "*intelligentia*," which, according to Aquinas' *Summa Theologica*, moved the planets.[5] As to who did move them—the devil knew only what he had heard at Oxford or Cambridge, where he was taught nothing but skepticism of the Ptolemaic tradition.[6] The heaven of the astronomers at Corpus Christi College, Cambridge, where Kit Marlowe was reading for his degree in 1583, was still pre-Copernican. It was Giordano Bruno who first spoke of Copernicus' doctrine in England in that same year. He defended the heliocentric view because the sun was more important than the earth, as Zoroaster and the Assyrians had been preaching for centuries. "There is the Magus announcing the Copernican theory in the context of the astral magic and sun worship of the *De Vita Coelitus Comparanda*."[7] The first great Magus of the Renaissance was Ficino.

These two heavens of the astrologers and astronomers over Cambridge and Wittenberg would not allow themselves to be separated for a long time. Two hells also hung over Cambridge and Wittenberg for quite a while.

> First will I question with thee about hell.

The German Faust was called "the insatiable speculator." Marlowe's *Faustus* was also most curious about the mysteries of heaven and hell.

> FAUSTUS: How many heavens or spheres are there?
> MEPHISTOPHILIS: Nine: the seven planets, the firmament, and the empyreal heaven:
> FAUSTUS: But is there not *coelum igneum? et crystallinum?*
> MEPHISTOPHILIS: No, Faustus, they be but fables.
> (2.2.58–62)

III

On the same title page of *The Tragicall History*, the devil extends a hairy paw to Faustus. He has a goatee, horns, black wings, and a corkscrew tail. He bears an uncanny resemblance to the Lucifer in *Queen Mary's Psalter*, and to the devil who tempts Christ in the thirteenth-century *Bible moralisée*. Lucifer appears in the same shape in the fourteenth- and fifteenth-century York plays. Among the props belonging to the Admiral's Men was a "dragon in fostes." But Faustus quickly chases this "dragon" from the medieval stage and tells the devil to change into monk's robes:

> Go, and return an old Franciscan friar.
> That holy shape becomes a devil best.
> (1.3.25–26)

In the German *Faustbuch*, Mephistophilis appears to Faustus as "a gray Friar." Luther believed in the devil. He had even seen him peering over his shoulder when he translated the Scripture into German in Wartburg Castle. And it was a devil in a frock. Protestants and even the great Melanchthon depicted the Catholic clergy as the devil's priests, and even saw a diable with a tail and cloven feet behind the Pope in Rome. "Why had not the Devil made a Pope of me?" wonders Faust in his Lutheran biography.

Marlowe borrowed the devil's monk's robes from the German *Faustbuch*, but his own dramatic discovery was to disguise the tempter as a Franciscan friar on stage. The "conjuror laureate," who attracts the "flowering pride of Wittenberg" to his lectures, disputes with a devil wearing monk's attire about the existence of hell.

> This word "damnation" terrifies me not,
> For I confound hell in elysium.
> My ghost be with the old philosophers.
> (1.3.58–60)

What an astonishing intellectual drama, utterly lost by modern directors, who like to depict Marlowe's Mephistophilis in the skimpy dress coat of Goethe's *Faust* or the red cape from the opera. The devil always appears in disguise, because otherwise he could frighten but not tempt. Even in the Garden of Eden, he took the guise of a serpent with a female head, according to an old and respectable tradition. But this pious disguise is the most sardonic. An unorthodox Doctor of Divinity convinces an orthodox devil that there is no hell: "Come, I think hell's a fable" (1.5.130). But who, if not the devil, would know that hell exists?

For a while it might seem that we are watching one of Shaw's comedies. But this Mephistophilis belongs to the late Renaissance, and this is the first tragic devil in the history of theater. "Why this is hell, nor am I out of it" (1.3.130). For the first time, hell is existential and there is "no exit" from its inner darkness. This is the hell which both Pascal and Kierkegaard will know well.

> But where we are is hell,
> And where hell is there must we ever be.
> (1.5.125–26)

But this is not the only hell in *Doctor Faustus*. "Enter Devils, giving crowns and rich apparel to Faustus; they dance and then depart" (stage direction 1.5.81). The spectators at early seventeenth-century performances well remembered the "shaggehayr'd Devills . . . roaring ouer the stage with Squibs in their mouthes, while Drummers make Thunder in the Tyringhouse, and the twelve-penny Hirelings make artificiall Lightning in their Heavens."[8] They were the same old demons who in the fourteenth-century York *Creation of Heaven and Earth* ran around whacking each other with sticks.[9]

This masque with its heavenly—or rather, infernal—fireworks with "thunder" and "lightning bolts" could be called the theater of Mephistophilis, just as the three spectacles in *The Tempest*—the initial storm, the banquet scene with disappearing food, and the last masque—might be called Ariel's shows. Interpreters have persistently defended Prospero against charges of black sorcery and have drawn subtle theological distinctions between the white magic of the exiled Duke of Milan and Faustus' conjuring of the devil. Faustus himself wants to be a "spirit in form and substance" in the pact to which Mephistophilis in turn must swear. "Thou art a spirit. God cannot pity thee" (2.2.13). But who is Ariel? Also "a spirit." Black as well as white magic, the manipulation of ways and means, seeks power through unlimited knowledge. The difference, if any, is not in the means, but only in the goals.

In *De civitate dei*, Augustine believes in demons, but these are not Socrates' *daemonion* who mediates between gods and men but ordinary devils or "wicked spirits."[10] Ariel in *The Tempest* would have been a "demon" in the hermetic tradition to the Neo-platonists, and one of the honest "spirits" to whom Pico turned for help, a mask for the devil to Augustine. In this theology, Caliban is, of course, an "evil spirit"—his father being a devil, his mother a witch. On his uninhabited isle, Prospero has only the good and evil spirits for company. But whether they are good or evil, all spirits are supposed to be obedient. Mephistophilis must execute Faustus' commands without objection, just as Ariel must be Prospero's obedient "slave" until he is freed.

PROSPERO: Hast, thou, spirit
    perform'd to point the tempest that I bade thee?
ARIEL: To every article.

(1.2.193–95)

The word "perform" is a theatrical term. In both plays, one hears it quite often. Mephistophilis and Ariel are the directors and main actors at the service of their masters. In *The Tempest* and *Doctor Faustus*, there is a theater within a theater with *two* separate audiences. Prospero attentively watches the spectacular storm which Ariel performs "to every article." He sits at "the top" watching as Ariel/Harpy performs tricks and snatches food and drink. In the last mythological masque, Prospero and the young couple sit in the first row of spectators.

Mephistophilis' circus is shown with full consciousness of the dramatic strategy as theater within a theater.

FAUSTUS: What means this show? Speak, Mephistophilis.
MEPHISTOPHILIS: Nothing, Faustus, but to delight thy mind,
    And let thee see what magic can perform.

(2.1.83–85)

At the next show of the diableries, Beelzebub himself will clearly announce: "Faustus, we are come from hell in person to show thee some pastime. Sit down . . ." (2.2.103–4).

The most perverse, ingenious, and still astonishing novelty of Marlowe was to show the Renaissance scholar as a spectator of the old morality play in which the medieval warlock, torn between good and evil angels, is tempted by the devils on his road to the grave. What a challenge for the directors; this alienated hell in the parody and reenactment of the medieval mystery play by the devil.

When Faustus demands that "the fairest maid in Germany" be brought to him, Mephistophilis is clearly enraged: "Marriage is but a ceremonial toy" (2.1.150). But in the cast of that diabolical performance, there is also a role for a "wife": "Enter a Devil dressed like a woman, with fireworks" (pyrotechnics are Mephistophilis' directorial specialty).

MEPHISTOPHILIS: Now Faustus, how dost thou like thy wife?
FAUSTUS: Here's a hot whore, indeed!

(2.1.148–49)

The next show is the parade of the Seven Deadly Sins, "led by a Piper," as in the morality plays from the lost *Ludus de Pater Noster* of the end of the fourteenth century to the best known, the *Castle of Perseveraunce*. They were well presented in the windows of gothic churches and in the allegorical wall paintings. Pride was shown at Ingatestone/Essex as "a richly dressed woman wearing a low-cut dress, seated upon a bench, or a coffer, while an attendant offered her a mirror."[11] In hell's pageant of *Doctor Faustus*, Pride is more ludicrous: "I can creep into every corner of a wench. Sometimes like a perevig I sit upon her brow. Next, like a necklace I hang about her neck. Then, like a fan of feathers, I kiss her . . ." (2.1.116 ff.).

At Ingatestone as well as in Mephistophilis' show, the Sins recall the ludicrous stories from sermons on the Devil's tricks and wiles. The Seven Deadly Sins are malicious and didactic. Envy, black and malodorous, "begotten of a chimneysweeper and an oyster wife," learned her jokes from Erasmus: "I cannot read and therefore wish all books were burnt" (lines 132 ff.). "Illiterate must dictate," wrote Stanislaw Jerzy Lec, the most brilliant of modern Polish aphorists three hundred years after Marlowe.[12] The Sins giggle, boast, and make obscene gestures almost as masques or costumed figures which could be seen in Polish villages during Shrovetide, or in New England during Halloween. Once again the pageant of the Seven Deadly Sins in *Faustus* comes from the carnival tradition. "O, how this sight doth delight my soul!" (3.2.163).

The protagonist of the first hell in *The Tragicall History* is a bitter and sad Mephistophilis, a sophisticated dialectician with the awareness of man in the twilight of the Renaissance. The protagonist of the second hell is the indefatigable and resourceful director, costume designer, and pyrotechnics expert. The two hells of *Doctor Faustus* are two different theaters.[13] The first hell, with its soliloquies and rhetorical and poetic tropes, marks the beginning of a tense and mature Elizabethan drama. The second is, at the same time, a parody and ingenious repetition of the medieval interludes, during which the folk devils tear the crown off Herod's head and drag him away. The first hell is discourse, the second is only a spectacle. The first hell is tragic, the second is farce, or, in terms closer to Marlowe's age, a burlesque and "mummery."

But to which of these two theaters does the scene with the selling of the soul and the signing of the pact with the devil belong? These would seem to be the most pathetic events in *The Tragicall History of Doctor Faustus*. The blood from the cut in Faustus' hand coagulates before he is able to sign with it. But Mephistophilis, taking care of everything, returns "with the chafer of fire." Faustus signs the pact with his own blood: "*consummatum est*: the bill is ended" (2.1.73).

Christ's last words on the cross, "It is finished," sound blasphemous on the lips of a man who has just signed a pact with the devil. And, undoubtedly, this is "blasphemy," but blasphemy with an old and respectable tradition. Religious hymns, the words of the Gospel, and liturgical tropes had been parodied from the early Middle Ages by monks and clerics. *Parodia sacra* and *risus paschalis* spared no hallowed text or sacred gesture. It was an old and time-honored custom, especially in the abbeys and parishes in the country. *Sacrum* and *profanum* were not divided, either in everyday life or on holy days. The Renaissance took over the parody of *sacra* from the Middle Ages. The greatest master of travesty of liturgical, legal, or medical texts was Rabelais. And it is not mere coincidence that Faustus' "blasphemy" appeared first in *Gargantua and Pantagruel*: in *Rabelais and His World*, Bakhtin wrote:

> Rabelais' Friar John is the incarnation of the mighty realm of travesty of the low clergy. He is a connoisseur of all that concerns the breviary (*en matière de brevière*): this means that he can reinterpret any sacred text in the sense of eating, drinking, and eroticism, and transpose it from the Lenten to the carnival "obscene" level . . . For instance, Christ's last words on the cross, *sitio*, "I thirst," and *consummatum est*, "it is consummated," are travestied into terms of eating and overindulgence. *Venite apotemus*, come and have a drink, replaced *venite adoremus*.[14]

The scene with the "chafer of fire" in which "the learned Faustus, fame of Wittenberg," signs the pact with the devil, belongs to the popular theater of a comic hell and immediately after the selling of the soul, which outwardly seems tragic and pathetic, a devilish circus takes place.

In the first scene of *The Tragicall History*, even before Mephistophilis is summoned, *serio* is mixed with *buffo*. Faustus sits and settles accounts with the books in his university study. First with Aristotle: "Sweet Analytics, 'tis thou has ravished me. */Bene disserere est finis logices*" (1.1.6–7). In the following verses the quotation turns openly ironic: "Is to dispute well logic's chiefest end?/Affords this art no greater miracle?" And again, in Greek: "Bid *on cai me on* farewell." A farewell to Aristotle's "being and non-being."

After philosophy comes the attack on medicine. Galen, famous in antiquity, is summoned: "*Summum bonum medicinae sanitas:/*The end of physic is our body's health." But medicine will not raise the dead and so is worth nothing. "Physic, farewell." Justinian is summoned after Galen. But Faustus has nothing but a mocking contempt for Roman law and its Latin maxims memorized at trivia:

> This study fits a mercenary drudge.
> Who aims at nothing but external trash.
> Too servile and illiberal for me.
>
> (1.1.33–35)

This violent repudiation of the traditional learning in the first soliloquy of Faustus was repeated after Cornelius Agrippa's *De vanitate scientiarum* (1526). Agrippa is present in *Doctor Faustus* at three different levels: as a character in drama under the name Cornelius who with Valdes (who may also have been a real person) visits Faustus in his study and encourages his black magic; as a historical person evoked in the dialogue ("I . . . will be as cunning as Agrippa was" [1.1.111, 116]); and, what is most important, as a model or double for Faustus himself.

One of the last Renaissance magi in the tradition of Ficino and Pico della Mirandola, Agrippa cultivated hermetic knowledge with a profound study of nature. After *De vanitate*, he wrote *De occulta philosophia*. Both treatises, translated in their day into Italian, French, and German, were published in several editions and widely read. In *De occulta*, Agrippa distinguished between natural magic, which was empirical science; mathematical magic, which operated in the planetary world; and a conjuration, sometimes called "ceremonial," which reached the supercelestial heaven, the realm of the spirits. With the power of the mind and through the secret incantations, one could not only draw forth feelings of love or hate at will, but one could also detect thieves, confuse columns of enemy armies, and summon storms, gales, and downpours.[15] Prospero could have had Agrippa's *De occulta* in his Milanese library. But while writing *The Tempest*, Shakespeare knew that the "carpenter" Inigo Jones was capable of producing tempests in the Blackfriars theater more spectacular than any magician's.[16]

In *De vanitate* both knowledge and magic were futile and empty. Agrippa ridicules in their turn grammar and dialectics, arithmetic and geometry, cosmography and astronomy, lullism or the art of remembering, poetry and music. Everything outside of the Divine Scripture was nothing but *vanitas vanitatum*. But Faustus ends his reenactment of Agrippa's *De vanitate* with an unexpected sneer: "Divinity, adieu!" Faustus' first great soliloquy, or rather the dialogue of the Renaissance scholar with old books, seems to belong, as Agrippa's *De vanitate*, to the long tradition of *serio ludere* almost as much as does the other contemporary masterpiece of mockery, *The Praise of Folly*. And that is how it was interpreted since the beginning.

In his *Defense of Poetry* (1595), Philip Sidney writes: "Agrippa will be as merry in showing the vanity of science as Erasmus was in the defending of folly. Neither shall any man or matter escape some touch of these smiling railers . . ." Faustus' contempt for the dead knowledge ends in the blasphemous challenge: "*Che serà, serà:*/What will be, shall be" (47–48). This first great soliloquy, studded with quotations and phrases in four languages, is a striking example of the *heteroglossia* of clowns and jesters described in Bakhtin as the source of the medieval and Renaissance fabliaux and street songs, "Where all 'languages' were masks and where no language could claim to be an authentic, incontestable face. . . . It was parodic, and aimed sharply and polemically against the official languages of its time: It was *heteroglossia* that had been dialogised."[17]

"Bid *on cai me on* farewell." "Physic, farewell." "Divinity, adieu!" To whom is Faustus bidding farewell in his university study? The *gay sciencia* of the Renaissance? No. He is saying adieu to the rubble of medieval disciplines and the theology which condemns all joy as a sad heritage of the Fall. Faustus sneers, as will Molière once again in the seventeenth century, at the arrogance of scholars, the ignorance of doctors, and the guile and subversion of lawyers.

The first teachers of this "sacred drôlerie" were Rabelais and Erasmus. Both, another chronological surprise, are contemporaries of the first German Fausts. One hears their sonorous laughter in this monologue, which neither interpreters from the Academia nor stage producers of *Doctor Faustus* seemed to have understood and praised.

Throughout the entire *Tragicall History*, at least from the first through fourth acts, *buffo* follows *serio*. After Faustus' incantations and the summoning of Mephistophilis, Wagner, Faustus' servant and pupil, threatens to change Clown, his hungry colleague, into a dog, cat, mouse, or rat. This poor fellow is always ready to sell his soul for "a shoulder of mutton . . . well roasted." But like Pride of the Seven Deadly Sins, Clown prefers to "tickle the pretty wenches' placket." In the interludes, "all he-devils has horns and all the she-devils has cliffs and cloven feet." Clown steals one of the magic books and, imitating his master, traces a magic circle. He does not know how to read and so spells the words, but even so he is efficient enough in his conjuring to summon Mephistophilis all the way from Constantinople.

In *serio ludere*, whose patrons in antiquity are Apuleius and Lucian, *serio* is *buffo* and *buffo* is *serio*. There is seriousness in the laughter and laughter in the seriousness. The high and the low, pedantry and superstition, the inflated and the shriveled, the dogma and the prejudice, the face and the mask, the refined and the vulgar, the learned and the rude, reflect and ape each other as in a funhouse mirror.

This medieval hell and the vulgar adventures of a folk magus have never been read from the perspective of carnival laughter and popular wisdom. Literary historians often express distaste for the lower genres. The scenes unworthy of the great dramaturge are gladly attributed to lesser writers. It is possible that many of the lines in the middle acts of *Faustus* are not from Marlowe's pen, but even if they are just hasty imitations of the *Faustbuch*, they are gold ore. *Doctor Faustus* remained an alive folk spectacle in innumerable ornate adaptations throughout Europe almost until the beginning of the nineteenth century. There must have been something powerful in this vulgar and naive spectacle. The young Goethe had seen his first *Faust* in the German puppet theater.

IV

Mephistophilis knew all the devils and subterfuges of the stage from the medieval interludes to the *commedia dell'arte* and the emergent Elizabethan theater. When Faustus decided to sneer at the Pope in Rome, Mephistophilis found him "a robe for to goo invisible" in the old prop room. Ariel dons the same "invisible-dress" when dispatched by Prospero on a special mission. The "invisible" Faustus has his irreverent jokes with the Pope, just as in *The Tempest* Ariel will play with Caliban and the drunken Stephano and Trinculo. Mephistophilis also finds a "false head" (4.3.37) in the old prop room, so that Benvolio, who seeks revenge, can "kill" Faustus. But the greatest "miracle" occurs when he summons the dead to the court of the German emperor. Faustus begins with a warning:

> My lord, I must forewarn your majesty
> That when my spirits present the royal shapes
> Of Alexander and his paramour.
> Your grace demand no question of the king,
> But in dumb silence let them come and go.
> (4.2.44–48)

When the fascinated emperor tears himself away from his seat to embrace Alexander's apparition, Faustus blocks his way and warns again, "These are but shadows, not substantial" (line 54). Mephistophilis advised Faustus to conjure up "spirits" by using the well-known device of the dumb show.[18] But perhaps the master of all devilry knew a more modern method of conjuring. In the first scene of act 1, Faustus predicts:

> And I . . .
> Will be as cunning as Agrippa was,
> Whose shadows made all Europe honour him.

What were these "shadows" which amazed the whole world? The narrator in Thomas Nashe's *The Unfortunate Traveler* (1594) had traversed Europe and met in Wittenberg "that abundant scholar," Agrippa, who was reputed "to be the greatest conjuror in Christendom." Agrippa then appears at the court of the emperor where he conjures up the destruction of Troy "in a dream," which is followed by the appearance of David, Gideon, and Solomon "in that similitude and likeness that they lived upon earth." The next night Agrippa showed Henry VIII and his lords hunting in Windsor forest "in a perspective glass."

What is this "perspective glass"? Undoubtedly a magic lantern with which Leonardo was apparently the first to experiment and whose striking effects were well known to sixteenth- and seventeenth-century magicians and conjurors.[19] Ariel in *The Tempest* had knowledge of the more subtle and sophisticated stage effects; the devilish director in *Doctor Faustus* with unquenched ambitions had to content himself with an old pantomime: "Music Sounds. Mephistophilis brings in Helen; she passeth over the stage" (stage direction 5.1.26).

The first apparition of Helen is to be viewed in fear: "Be silent then, for danger is in words" (5.1.25). In a similar manner, Prospero warns Ferdinand and Miranda at the start of the masque in *The Tempest*: "No tongue! all eyes! be silent" (4.1.59). But the Helen who appears for the second time in *Doctor Faustus* is no longer a shadow without substance. Faustus holds her in his arms. In a modern theater where the traditions and conventions of the pre-Elizabethan and Elizabethan stage have been lost, Marlowe's astonishing ingenuity can be entirely overlooked. The convention of the "dumb show" is violated. The apparition has become flesh. And it is then that Faustus speaks two lines which will forever remain in English poetry:

> Was this the face that launched a thousand ships
> And burnt the topless towers of Ilium?
>   (5.1.99–100)

The classical source of these lines is Lucian's *Dialogues of the Dead*—one of the most amazing incidents in the whole history of literature is Lucian's co-authorship with Marlowe and Shakespeare. The same few lines are also the source of another scene, one of the most memorable in Renaissance drama:[20]

Alexander died, Alexander was buried, Alexander returneth to dust, is earth, of earth we make him loam. and why of that loam whereto he was converted might they not stop a beer-barrel?

(*Hamlet* 5.1.194–98)

Lucian's *Dialogues of the Dead* take place in hell. Hermes shows the newly arrived Menippus around Hades.

MENIPPUS: Hermes, where are all the handsome men and beautiful women? Show me the sights: I've just arrived.
HERMES: I am busy now, Menippus. Just look over there, on the right. You'll find Hyacinth, Narcissus, Nireus, Achilles, Tyro, Helen, Leda—in short, all the great beauties of long ago.
MENIPPUS: All I can see are bones and skulls without any flesh on them. Most of them look alike.
HERMES: Well, these bones that you seem to look down your nose at are what all the poets have been raving about.
MENIPPUS: Show me Helen's head anyway. I could hardly pick it out by myself.
HERMES: This one is Helen.
MENIPPUS: Well! Is this what launched a thousand ships from every part of Greece, and was responsible for slaughtering so many Greeks and Trojans and destroying so many cities?
HERMES: Ah, Menippus, you never saw her in the flesh.[21]

In this Greek Hades, the skulls and bones lie scattered in a common ditch. Lucian's hell, hallucinating and horrifying, imprinted itself on the memories of both Shakespeare and Marlowe, who had read *Dialogues of the Dead* as schoolboys. From ancient times to the late Renaissance, Alexander was the image of human greatness,[22] while Helen personified beauty. In the mass grave history remains nameless, the bones cannot be distinguished, and nothing remains but the stench.

HAMLET: Dost thou think Alexander looked o' this fashion i' the earth?
HORATIO: E'en so.
HAMLET: And smelt so? puh!

(5.1.184–86)

Faustus conjures Alexander's shadow for the German emperor, for himself "to glut the longing of my heart's desire" (5.1.6) asks Mephistophilis to conjure Helen. But "heavenly Helen," who Faustus holds in his arms and kisses, in this blend of the concrete and the symbolic, is at the same time an apparition and flesh, a ghost and a succubus, as much pagan myth as Christian nightmare.

> Her lips suck forth my soul: see where it flies
> Come, Helen, come . . .
>
> (1.1.100–101)

Helen of sex and metaphysics sucks out both the marrow and the soul. And she will never return the body and soul she comes to possess. Her immortality is the ashes of cities. All Troys burn in Marlowe and Shakespeare, just as they burned in Homer and Virgil. And in each new Troy, there is a new face of Helen:

> I will be Paris and for love of thee
> Instead of Troy shall Wittenberg be sack'd.
>
> (1.1.106–7)

Once again one can hear this rare voice of an undisguised and penetrating confession: "And all is dross that is not Helena" (line 103). All of us who are old enough know: life with Helen is a disaster, but life without Helen is a void.

This deadly Helen appears, almost at the same time, in the final stanzas of Thomas Nashe's *Summer's Last Will and Testament*. Summer dies, but this is a summer of impending plague.

> The plague full swift goes by;
> I am sick, I must die;
>   Lord, have mercy on us.
>
> Beauty is but a flower,
> Which wrinkles will devour,
> Brithness falls from the air.
> Queens have died young and fair,
> Dust hath clos'd Helen's eye.
> I am sick, I must die;
>   Lord, have mercy on us.[23]

At the close of the Renaissance, Helen is a sign and omen of doom.

V

In a moment the clock will strike eleven. Faustus has but one hour left before he dies. Out of the theatrical "heavens" there is "Music while the throne descends" (stage direction 5.2.108). In one moment later "the jaws of hell" (line 126), breathing fire, emerge from the trap room. In Elizabethan theater, the "throne" from the heavens descended only one more time in a now-forgotten play, and no other source mentions "the jaws of hell" again after *Doctor Faustus*.[24]

For the Elizabethan spectator, these two anachronistic emblems were not the imagining and summoning of Heaven and Hell, but of the medieval "heaven" and the medieval "hell" of the old, almost forgotten theater. From the early medieval York cycle to the late medieval *Everyman*, the theology and dramatic action of all the mystery and morality plays is the path from damnation to salvation in the history of mankind and the life of everyman. Christ, the second Adam, leads the first Adam out of purgatory, as in *The Harrowing of Hell*. There are only two exceptions to this theological and dramatic rule: Cain, whose "synne it passis al mercie," and later Judas.[25] The morality play always ends with the salvation of the sinner. *The Tragicall History of Doctor Faustus* ends with eternal damnation.

> Damned art thou, Faustus, damned: despair and die!
> Hell claims his right . . .
>
> (5.1.56–57)

The morality play became an anti-morality play. The message of the Christian morality play is inverted and negated in *Doctor Faustus*. Despair—*desperatio*—signifies loss of hope, even in the root of the word. Despair, a sin against the Holy Spirit, a lack of faith in God's mercy, and a lack of faith in salvation, is the consciousness of death everlasting in desperation. "Despair and die!"[26]

Marlowe's *Faustus* has often been called a tragedy of despair. The words "despair" and "desperate" appear thirteen times in this play. Even before Faustus summons Mephistophilis, we hear of a "desperate maladie" and "desperate enterprise." Later there are "desperate thoughts" and "desperate steps," and, the most modern, "desperate lunacy."

The first great magus of Renaissance tragedy is Faustus. The last is Prospero. In *The Tempest*, the word "despair" appears at the very end, in the sixth verse before the last line, in that farewell monologue of Prospero's spoken directly to the spectators: "And my ending is despair,/Unless I be reliev'd by prayer." But Marlowe's Faustus knows that no prayers will be able to keep the yawning gates of hell at bay: "I do repent and yet I do despair" (5.1.71). Man must die; there is no getting around it. "What art thou, Faustus, but a man condemned to die?" (4.5.22). Faustus dies in despair.

"I'll burn my books!" are his last words. The other great conjurer also renounces his art:

> I'll break my staff,
> Bury in certain fathoms in the earth,
> And deeper than did ever plummet sound
> I'll drown my book.
>
> (5.2.61–64)

The bitterness of both of these late Renaissance magi is the loss of hope. All hope. Neither Art, nor Magic, nor Knowledge is capable of changing the world. The serpent in Paradise imposed an illusion of hope: "ye shall be as gods." This late Renaissance Satan is a teacher of despair. The despair in *Faustus* and the despair of Faustus are not simply Christian, but only a Christian despair has created a language rich enough in emotional tension and metaphysics to express the despair of unbelievers as well. It is not just a Christian hell that contains no hope. Marlowe knew this as perhaps none of his contemporaries did. Nor is this hell just a personal, private one. It is a hell of history without hope or salvation. Marlowe's hell may be our hell, too.

Mephistophilis carries hell within himself. This was Marlowe's greatest dramatic discovery, even if he did borrow it from Aquinas. But this is not merely a hell of despair. It is also a hell of transgression and rebellion. Faustus rejects God who had rejected him. "To God? He loves thee not." The message of the medieval mystery play is once again inverted.

The only mythical figures of the new epoch, which began with the Renaissance, are Faust and Don Juan. They have a different darkness within themselves and carry various hells, but both have eaten the forbidden fruit from the tree of knowledge. The price of cognition is hell, but the price of delight is another hell.

In Thomas Kyd's *Spanish Tragedy*, staged in 1592, the same year as *Doctor Faustus*, the avenger tells of "monstrous times" when "the soul delights in interdicted things." Faustus and Don Juan know by the senses and by intellect the delight of transgression. The great teacher of this delight is ever Lucifer. He discloses a truth, one which twentieth-century literature will repeatedly rediscover: "But Faustus, in hell is all manner of delight." Marlowe himself must have been acquainted with this truth or even more with this experience, as Faustus' lines have a personal tone not found in any of his other plays, nor even in any of Shakespeare's dramas, except *The Tempest*. In a strange way, both Faust and Don Juan from the end of the Renaissance, who know so well that hell is the price of knowledge and joy, do not cease being contemporary heroes from at least the second half of the eighteenth century to the end of our own.

"The Renaissance magus turned into Faust," suggested Frances Yates.[27] But into what kind of Faust? Into the folk sorcerer who advertised himself as a "fountain of necromancers, astrologer, magus secundus, chiromancer, aromancer, pyromancer, second in hydromancy,"[28] and whom, shortly after his death, the Lutherans and Jesuits alternately joined to Agrippa and accused of being "ignoble conjurers," whom the devil always accompanied in the shape of a black dog? (This "black poodle [*der schwarze Pudel*]" was to reappear in Goethe's *Faust*.) Or perhaps into that rotund and complacent astrologer from the title page of *The Tragicall History*, to whom an old-fashioned dragon extends his hairy paw? Or maybe into the Faust from Rembrandt's etching which depicts him as the personification of the new Melancholy? But what sort of face does Marlowe's Faustus have?

Marlowe, one of the most radical and independent minds of his day, believed neither in guardian angels nor in the conjuring of spirits, and that is why Faustus sells his soul among the "diableries" of the devils' comic theater. But this comic theater is just one part of *The Tragicall History of the Life and Death of Doctor Faustus*.

Bakhtin has often written about the dialogic nature of thought and truth, which appeared most fully in the literature which stemmed from the Saturnalia and the carnival tradition. The linguistic expression of this dialogue is polyphony, Bakhtin's *heteroglossia*—meetings and matings at the marketplace, where idiolects and idioms, slang and dialects, the most various social tongues, each bring a different experience, different beliefs and customs, different vision and understanding.

"Dialogue" and "dialogization" are the basic principles, indeed the essence, of a novel. But not of drama. For Bakhtin, a dramatic dialogue does not have the "carnival polyphony," the multiple voices, the encounter between various experiences in "their own" separate tongues. But polyphony, the meeting of various experiences, of various "ways of speaking," may appear not in the dialogue of characters but in the "dialogue" of various "theaters," of various theatrical forms in one play. "Polyphony" is then "polytheatricality," polymorphics are stage polygraphics.

In this sense, Marlowe's *Faustus* is a great "polytheatrical" drama. Theaters and spectacles appear in it as dramatis personae, who speak with their own, various and independent "voices": tragic discourse in blank verse; the anachronistic morality of the late Middle Ages; interludes with ribald jokes and coarse humor; the masques and antimasques; the dumbshow; Italian *lazzi* from the *commedia dell'arte,* the parody of liturgical rites and exorcisms; and even metaphysical poetry, as in Faustus' last soliloquy, the tension of whose religious horror, its *tremendum,* can challenge that in Donne's poems.

In all these stages, not only are all of Faustus' fascinating and repugnant faces shown, but we also get—as in none of the other masterpieces of the Renaissance and Baroque drama except perhaps Shakespeare's *Hamlet*, Tirso de Molina's *El Burlador de Sevilla*, and Calderón's *Life Is a Dream*—a sense of man's predicament at the threshold of the seventeenth century. This bitter vision could not be arranged into a harmonious whole because of its violent internal contradictions. The Renaissance magus' hopes of penetrating the mysteries of the heavens turned out to be illusory, and even more illusory were the philosophers' hopes for the coming of a kingdom of reason and freedom. Giordano Bruno was thrown into the dungeons of the Holy Office in 1592, the same year in which Marlowe wrote *Doctor Faustus*.[29]

"O, would I had never seen Wittenberg, never read a book" (5.2.46). This was not a victory for Mephistophilis but for the small, envious, and hateful devils in the hoods of the Holy Inquisition.

The Tragicall History of the Life and Death of Doctor Faustus has two endings. In the first, Faustus is found lying on the floor, his limbs mangled, "all torn asunder by the hand of death" (5.3.7): an old warning not "to practice more than heavenly power permits" (epilogue, line 8).[30] But there is also another ending:

> Yet, for he was a scholar, once admir'd
> For wondrous knowledge in our German schools,
> We'll give his mangled limbs due burial;
> And all the students, clothed in mourning black,
> Shall wait upon his heavy funeral.

This is the first lay funeral in the entire history of drama. Hamlet's body was carried on the shoulders of soldiers. The performance of *Tragicall History* should end with a procession of Faustus' friends and students bearing his body from his study in Wittenberg.

Marlowe did not have such a funeral. On May 30, 1593, he was stabbed "over his right eye" with a dagger. Like Faustus, he lay face down on the floor. The murder had been ordered by the powerful of that world. Embroiled in many sordid affairs, Marlowe was too well known to be a blasphemer and atheist.

Seven years later a pamphlet appeared which claimed that the death of Marlowe, just like that of Faustus, was divine punishment: "Thus did God the true executioner of divine justice, invoke the end of an impious atheist."[31]

That same year, Hamlet's words to the two royal spies, Rosencrantz and Guildenstern, rang from the Elizabethan stage:

> What a piece of work is man! how noble in reason! how infinite
> in faculties! in form and moving, how express and admirable!

in actions, how like an angel! in apprehension, how like a god!
the beauty of the world; the paragon of the animals! And yet
to me what is this quintessence of dust? Man delights not me—
not, nor woman neither . . .

(2.2.319–24)

Translated by Lillian Vallee

Notes

1. Frances A. Yates, *The Occult Philosophy in the Elizabethan Age* (London: Routledge, 1979), p. 17.

2. Tamburlaine tears the crowns from the heads of kings he has defeated and throws them on the stage. These "crowns" appear thirty-five times in part 1. In *Edward II*, the word "crown" appears twenty-three times. In *The Jew of Malta*, gold "crowns" appear twenty-eight times, five more than in *Edward II*. All quotations are from *Christopher Marlowe: The Complete Plays*, ed. J. B. Steane (New York: Penguin, 1969).

3. Lynn Thorndike, *A History of Magic and Experimental Science* (New York: Columbia University Press, 1923), 7:8: "Newton left nothing in print on the subject of alchemy, but alchemy is the leading interest of over a million words left in his own handwriting." See also ibid., 8:240.

4. I am quoting from the translation of E. L. Forbes in *The Renaissance Philosophy of Man* (Chicago, 1948).

5. In hermetic tradition each of the heavenly bodies "is in turn controlled by demons, and . . . it is the 'governors' of the seven planets who are especially powerful." See Peter J. French, *John Dee: The World of an Elizabethan Magus* (London: Routledge & Kegan Paul, 1972), p. 70.

6. Frances R. Johnson, "Marlowe's Astronomy and Renaissance Skepticism," *ELH* 13 (1946): 241: "Faustus poses and Mephistophilis answers, the chief questions of sixteenth-century philosophical debate concerning the structure and motions of the heavens. . . . The playwright raises problems inspired by the disagreement among the astronomical textbooks then current at Cambridge, and has the answers given by Mephistophilis accord with the doctrine expounded by the unconventional rather than the more orthodox authorities."

7. Frances A. Yates, *Giordano Bruno and the Hermetic Tradition* (London: Routledge, 1964), pp. 208 ff.

8. John Melton (1620), cited by John Bakeless in *The Tragicall History of Christopher Marlowe* (Hamden, Conn.: Archon Books, 1964), p. 298.

9. See Clifford Davidson, *From Creation to Doom: The York Cycle of Mystery Plays* (New York, AMS Press, 1984), p. 33.

10. See Yates, *Occult Philosophy*, p. 10.

11. M. D. Anderson, *Drama and Imagery in English Medieval Churches* (Cambridge, 1963), pp. 60 ff. During Marlowe's time at Manningtree there were still the fairs and charters by yearly stage plays, and Thomas Nashe (who was in so many instances involved with *Doctor Faustus*) wrote in *The Choice of Valentine* of "a play of strange moralitie/Shoven by the bachelrie of Manning-tree/Where to the countrie franklins flock-meale swarme."

12.   Stanislaw Jerzy Lec (1909–56), the brilliant Polish aphorist who could be compared only to Karol Kraus. See his *Unkempt Thoughts* (New York: St. Martin's Press, 1962), p. 157.

13.   This juxtaposition of the two different visions of hell exists in the German *Faustbuch*: "in this confused hell is nought to find but a filthy, sulphurish, fiery, stinking mist or fog. . . . Further, we Devils know not how God hath laid the foundation of our hell, nor whereof it is: but to be short . . . we know that hell hath neither bottom nor end." See *The Historie of the Damnable Life and Deserved Death of Doctor Faustus*, ed. W. K. Pfeiler (Notre Dame: University of Notre Dame Press, 1963), pp. 84–85. Compare this with Marlowe's "hell hath no limits, nor is circumscribed/In one self place" (2.1.119–20). Marlowe made two opposing theaters of this opposition of two "hells."

14.   Mikhail Bakhtin, *Rabelais and His World* (Cambridge, Mass.: MIT Press, 1968), p. 86.

15.   Agrippa, *Occult Philosophy*, 2.168–69: "A Magus, expert in naturall philosophy, and Mathematics, and knowing the middle sciences, consisting of bothe these, Arithmatick, Musick, Geometry, Optics, Astronomie, and such sciences that are of weights, measures, proportions, articles and joynts, knowing also Mechanicall Arts resulting from these, may without any wonder, if he excell other man in Art, and wit, do many wonderful things . . ." I am quoting from French, p. 108.

16.   Mikhail Bakhtin, *The Dialogic Imagination: Four Essays*, ed. Michael Holquist (Austin, Texas: University of Texas Press, 1981), p. 27.

17.   Inigo Jones, with his use of *periaktoi* and *machina versatilis* could have easily produced the illusion of the storm in the prologue of *The Tempest*. In Ben Jonson's *Masque of Blackness* performed in the *Banqueting House* in 1605, or six years before *The Tempest*, "an artificiall sea was seen to shoot forth, as it flowed to the land, raysed with waves, which seemed to move, and in some places the billow to break, as imitating that *orderly disorder* which is common in nature. . . . The *Masquers* were placed in a great concave shell, like mother of pearle, curiously made to move on those waters and rise with the billow" (Ben Jonson, *Works*, ed. C. H. Herford and Percy and Evelyn Simpson, 11 vols. [Oxford: Clarendon Press, 1925–52], 7:170–71). In 1632 James Shirley described in *Loves Crueltie* the theatrical illusions created by Jones: "a tempest so artificiall and suddaine in the clouds, with a generall darkness and thunder so seeming made to threaten, that you would cry out with the Marriners . . ." Quoted from Stephen Orgel and Roy Strong, *Inigo Jones: The Theatre of the Stuart Court* (Berkeley: University of California Press, 1973), p. 15.

18.   In *Gorboduc* (1561–62), the first English tragedy written in blank verse, each act ends with a "dumb-show" that anticipates the events that follow. In *The Arraignment of Paris* (1581–82), the earliest of the preserved pastorals with music and songs, Helen, in the Venus' Show, "Ent'reth in her bravery, with four Cupids attending on her, each having his fan in his hand to fan fresh air in her face." Helen's second entrance in *Faustus* appears to repeat this "dumb-show" from *The Arraignement of Paris*: "Enter Helen again, passing over [the stage] between two Cupids." The "dumb-show" appears in Shakespeare at least three times: in *Hamlet* in the co-

medians' first pantomime, "Gonzago's Murder"; in *Macbeth* in the dumb-show of the future kings of Scotland; and in *The Tempest* in the scene with Ariel/Harpy. Webster used the "dumb-show" for the spectacles of terror in *The White Devil* and *The Duchess of Malfi*.

19. Cornelis Drebbel (1572–1633) was probably the most secretive and magical figure in the scientific and technical world of the early seventeenth century. Drebbel "could make a flat sheet of glass without any ground edge, in which one could see one's face seven times. . . . He asserted that his magic lantern would show him not only in different colors, but in the form of a tree or animal, and Constantyn Huygens, father of the famous physicist, wrote on March 17, 1622, that Drebbel's *camera obscura* was certainly one of the chief features of his sorcery. . . . Drebbel is also said to have shown likenesses of persons who were not present and to have devised an incubator" (Thorndike, 7:496).

20. See W. S. Heckscher, "Was this the face . . .?", *Journal of the Warburg and Courtauld Institutes* 2 (1937–38): 295–97.

21. *Selected Satires of Lucian*, ed. and trans. Lionel Casson (New York: W. W. Norton, 1958), p. 205.

22. Compare Don Juan's ironic comparison of himself to Alexander in Molière: "I felt it is in me to love the whole world, and like Alexander still wish for new worlds to conquer" (act 1, sc. 2). And once again in the scene with Elvira: "Madame: We left because of Alexander and the other worlds he still had to conquer" (act 1, sc. 3).

23. This Helen (of whom only ashes remain, too) appears even closer to its source in Lucian if one reads "from the *air*" as "from the *hair*." "Other suggestions, beyond enumeration, are present also." See C. L. Barber, *Shakespeare's Festive Comedy* (Cleveland, 1959), p. 82. Another suggestion "beyond enumeration" is the sexual innuendo in "queens." See also Nashe's *The Terrors of the Night* (1593): "Therefore was Troy burnt by night, because Paris by night prostituted Helena." And even in one of Orlando's naive verses we find, "Nature presently distilled/ Helen's cheek, but not heart" (*As You Like It* 3.2.147–48).

24. The "throne" which descends from the heavens in *Faustus* and in *A Looking Glass for London and England*, the "creaking throne" scorned by Jonson, which Henslowe notes as being stored in the heavens, was a chair for flights and nothing else quite different from the "state." See A. Gurr, *The Shakespearean Stage, 1547–1642* (London, 1971), p. 127. "Ugly Hell, gape not" (*Faustus* 5.3.119) appears for the first time in the oldest surviving miracle play in England, *The Creation of the World*: "Let Hell gape when the Father names it" (stage direction line 244).

25. In *Sacrificium Cayme and Abell* in the Chester plays. See Davidson, p. 48.

26. The word "despair" appears some sixty times in Shakespeare. On most of the occasions, "despair" comes in the context of suicidal death, and, therefore, in Christian theology, carried with it the certainty of going to hell, as, for example, in *Richard III*, in Richard's scene with Anne: "ANNE. No excuse . . . but to hang yourself. RICHARD. By such despair I should accuse myself" (1.2.84–85). Special attention should be drawn to what is probably taken from *Faustus*, the phrase "despair and die" (which is re-

peated nine times) in the scene where the ghosts of the murdered appear to Richard the night before the battle (act 5, sc. 8). "Despair and die!" means simply "die and go to hell." At the end of the curse of Buckingham's Ghost, for example, we find, "And die in terror of thy guiltiness!/ Dream on, dream on, of bloody deeds and death:/ Fainting, despair; despairing, yield thy breath!" (5.3.170 ff.). Among the last words Richard utters in this scene is the same sentence as in *Faustus*: "I shall despair" (line 200).

27.   Frances Yates's interpretation (that Marlowe joined the Counterreformation "witch hunters" in *Doctor Faustus* by presenting the Renaissance magus as a "warlock") is a mistaken and oversimplified reading of the drama. Sometimes even the greatest intellectual historians are incapable of deciphering theatrical signs. For them drama is only a printed text.

28.   See Frank Baron, *Doctor Faustus: From History to Legend* (Munich: Fink Verlag, 1978), pp. 31 ff. Rabelais had already been laughing at sorcerers in *Gargantua* (when Panurge goes for advice to Herr Trippa): "you know how, through the arts of astrology, geomancy, chiromancy, metomancy, and others of the same gest, he predicts all things to come" (3.25). Even in the second half of the seventeenth century, Samuel Butler in his *Hudibras*, one of the last works in the tradition of *serio ludere*, mocked believers in sorcery and magic (see *Hudibras*, ed. J. Wilders [Oxford, 1967]):

> Agrippa kept a Stygian-Pig,
> I' th'garb and habit of a Dog,
> That was his Tutor; and the Curr
> Read to th'Occult Philosopher,
> And taught him subtly to maintain
> All other Sciences are vain.
>
> To this, quoth Sidrophello, Sir,
> Agrippa was no Conjurer,
> Not Paracelsus, no nor Behman;
> Nor was the Dog a Cacodaemon,
> But a true Dog, that would shew tricks,
> For th'Emperor, and leap o'er sticks;
> Would fetch and carry, was more civil
> Then other Dogs, but yet no Devil . . .
> (2.3.635 ff.)

29.   Bruno was burned at the stake in the year 1600. The history of the text is not the subject of this essay, but it is worth noting that in the 1616 edition, Faustus, dressed as a cardinal in the scene with the Pope, announces the sentence of the Holy Council on Bruno, the anti-Pope recognized by the German emperor: "He shall be straight condemn'd of heresy/And on a pile of faggots burnt to death" (3.1.183–84).

30.   The inner contradictions in legend and in Marlowe's drama are shown very clearly by Don Ihde: "Faustus wants the power—knowledge to heal, to work wonders over the material, to exercise and manipulate events and even Nature. . . . The very utopian hope turns to be a temptation of the sort which leads to a Fall. . . . There is, in Faustus, the identification of knowledge-power with the hubris of wanting to become a god, an echo of one of the Garden story possibilities. And implicitly, there is in Faustus the

subterranean nostalgia for remaining intuitively placed within Nature, not exceeding its bounds. To do so tempts the gods and threatens the very position of humans. Faustus is the inversion, the dystopian underside of Baconian utopianism." *Consequences of Phenomenology* (Albany: State University of New York Press, 1986), p. 99.

31.   See Irving Ribner, *The Complete Plays of Christopher Marlowe* (New York: Odyssey Press, 1963), p. xx.

The Bottom Translation

I

"Love looks not with the eyes, but with the mind" (1.1.234).[1] This soliloquy of Helena's is part of a discourse on love and madness. Does desire also look with "the mind" and not with "the eyes"? Titania awakens from her dream, looks at the monster, and desires him. When Lysander and Demetrius awaken, they see only a girl's body and desire it. Is desire "blind" and love "seeing"? Or is love "blind" and desire "seeing"? "And therefore is wing'd Cupid painted blind" (1.1.235). Puck is the culprit in *A Midsummer Night's Dream*, for he awakens desire by dropping a love potion into the eyes of the sleeping lovers. In the poetic rhetoric of *A Midsummer Night's Dream*, "blind Cupid" is the agent of love. Are Puck and Cupid interchangeable?

Helena's soliloquy is recited by a young actress or, as in Elizabethan theater, by a boy acting the woman's part. The soliloquy is the voice of the actor. But it is not, or not only, the voice of the *character*. It is a part of a polyphonic, or many-voiced, discourse on love. In *A Midsummer Night's Dream* this discourse is more than the poetic commentary to the events taking place onstage. And the action onstage is more than illustration of the text. The discourse and the action not only complement each other but also appear to contradict each other. The dramatic tension and the intellectual richness result from this confrontation of discourse and action.

The same similes and emblems recur from the first to the last act of the play. *Emblem* may be the most appropriate term, for Cupid is the most significant image in this discourse. This "child" (1.1.238), "the boy Love" (1.1.241), waggish, fore-swearing, and beguiling, repeats the post-classical icon of the blind or blindfolded Cupid.

From the early medieval poem, "I am blind and I make blind" to Erasmus' *Praise of Folly*, the icon is constant: "But why is Cupide alwaies lyke a yonge boie? why? but that he is a trifler, neither doyng, nor thynkyng any wyse acte" (20.20).[2] But this blind or blindfolded Cupid, associated in the Middle Ages with personifications of evil and darkness—Night, Infidelity, and Fortune—became by the Renaissance a sign with two contradictory values set in semiotic opposition. "Blind" Cupid does "see," but only at night, as in one of the most evocative lines in Marlowe's *Hero and Leander*, "dark night is Cupid's day"; or, once again he "sees" but "with an incorporeal eye," as in Pico della Mirandola.[3] This second Cupid, blind but seeing "with the mind," appears soon after the first in Helena's soliloquy:

> Things base and vile, holding no quantity,
> Love can transpose to form and dignity.
> (1.1.232–33)

Who and what is spoken of? Hermia, who is "sweet" and "fair," is hardly "base and vile." Helena does not know yet that Hermia is soon to be her rival. The "real" Helena, a character in the comedy, cannot here be referring to Hermia. The voice of the actor speaking of the madness of Eros forecasts Titania's infatuation with the "monster." But not only Bottom was "translated" that night. "Bless thee, Bottom, bless thee! Thou art translated" (3.1.113). "Translation" was the word used by Ben Jonson for metaphor. But in Shakespeare, "translation" is the sudden discovery of desire. Both couples of young lovers were "translated": "Am I not Hermia? Are you not Lysander?" (3.2.273). Bottom's metamorphosis is only the climax of the events in the forest. This "night-rule" (3.2.5) ends immediately after Bottom's return to human shape. Oberon and Titania "vanish." Theseus and Hippolyta return with the beginning of the new day in place of their night doubles. The lovers wake up from their "dream." And Bottom too wakes up from his: "I have had a dream, past the wit of man to say what dream it was. Man is but an ass if he go about to expound this dream . . . The eye of man hath not heard, the ear of man hath not seen, man's hand is not able to taste, his tongue to conceive, nor his heart to report, what my dream was" (4.1.204–6, 209–12).

The source of these astonishing lines is well known. "It must be accepted," wrote Frank Kermode in his *Early Shakespeare* (1961), "that this is a parody of 1 Corinthians 2:9–10": "Eye hath not seen, nor ear heard, neither have entered into the heart of man the things which God hath prepared for them that love him. But God hath revealed *them* unto us by his Spirit: for the Spirit searcheth all things, yea, the deep things of God."

Kermode quoted the King James version. In Tyndale (1534) and in the Geneva New Testament (1557) the last verse reads, "the Spirite searcheth all thinges, ye the botome of Goddes secrettes."[4] The "Athenian" weaver probably inherited his name from Paul's letter in old versions of Scripture. The spirit which reaches to "the botome" of all mysteries haunts Bottom. But just "translated" into an ass, Bottom translates Paul in his own way: "I will get Peter Quince to write a ballad of this dream: it shall be called 'Bottom's Dream,' because it hath no bottom" (4.1.212–15).

But Bottom was not the only one in *A Midsummer Night's Dream* to read 1 Corinthians. We find another echo of Paul's letter in Helena's soliloquy:

> Things base and vile, holding no quantity,
> Love can transpose to form and dignity.

Paul had written, "And base things of the world, and things which are despised, hath God chosen, *yea,* and things which are not to bring to naught things that are" (1 Cor. 1:28). In Tyndale and in the Geneva Bible this verse starts, "and vile thinges of the worlde." "Things base," in Helena's lines, appears to be borrowed from the Geneva Bible, and "vile" repeats the wording of the Authorized Version.

For an interpreter a "text" does not exist independently of its readings. Great texts, and perhaps even more so quotations from classical texts, literal or parodistic, form, together with their readings, a literary and cultural tradition. The classical texts are constantly rewritten, they are "the writerly text," to use Barthes's term.[5] Interpretations and commentaries become a part of their life. Classical texts and quotations continuously repeated are active in intellectual *emanation* which gives them new meaning and changes old ones. This emanation is the history of the classical text as well as the history hidden in the literary text. Classical texts converse among themselves. But borrowings and quotations are never neutral. Each quotation enlists its own context to challenge the author's text for better understanding or for mockery. The literary tradition, "the writerly text," works forward and backward, constructing and destroying the classical texts, illuminating or disintegrating them, consecrating or desecrating, or both. The literary history is, in a very literal sense, the eating and digesting of the classical texts.

The verse from Corinthians parodied by Bottom and the biblical "things base and vile" in Helena's lines refer to Bottom's transformation and to Titania's sudden infatuation with the monster—both borrowed from Apuleius' *The Golden Ass*. Shakespeare might have read Apuleius in Latin or in Adlington's translation of 1566.[6] The riddle of *A Midsummer Night's Dream* is not only why Paul or Apuleius was evoked in it but also why *both* were evoked and involved in the dramatic nexus of Bottom's metamorphosis.

Both texts, Corinthians and *The Golden Ass*, were widely known, discussed, and quoted during the Renaissance. From the early sixteenth century until the late seventeenth century, both texts were read in two largely separate intellectual traditions having two discrete circuits, and interpreted in two codes which were complementary but contradictory. The first of these codes, which is simultaneously a tradition, a system of interpretation, and a "language," can be called Neoplatonic or hermetic. The second is the code of the carnival or, in Mikhail Bakhtin's terms, the tradition of *serio ludere*.

> The carnival attitude possesses an indestructible vivacity and the mighty, life-giving power to transform. . . . For the first time in ancient literature the object of a *serious* (though at the same time comical) representation is presented without epical

or tragical distance, presented not in the absolute past of myth and legend, but on the contemporary level, in direct and even crudely familiar contact with living contemporaries. In these genres mythical heroes and historical figures out of the past are deliberately and emphatically contemporarized . . .

The serio-comical genres are not based on *legend* and do not elucidate themselves by means of the legend—they are *consciously* based on *experience* and on *free imagination;* their relationship to legend is in most cases deeply critical, and at times bears the cynical nature of the expose. . . . They reject the stylistic unity. . . . For them multiplicity of tone in a story and a mixture of the high and low, the serious and the comic, are typical: they made wide use . . . of parodically reconstructed quotations. In some of these genres the mixture of prose and poetic speech is observed, living dialects and slang are introduced, and various authorial masks appear.[7]

II

Paul's letter to the Corinthians is often invoked in the writings of Neoplatonists. In Mirandola, Ficino, Leone Ebreo, and Bruno, Paul can be found next to the Sibyl of the *Aeneid,* King David, Orpheus, Moses, or Plato. For the hermetics and Florentine philosophers, as for Lévi-Strauss, "myths rethink each other in a certain manner" ("d'une certaine manière, les mythes se pensent entre eux").[8] While icons and signifiers are borrowed from Plato and Plotinus, Heraclitus and Dionysius the Areopagite, the Psalms, Orphic hymns and cabalistic writings, the signified is always one and the same: the One beyond Being, unity in plurality, the God concealed. At times the method of the Neoplatonists resembles strangely the belief of poststructuralism and the new hermeneutics—that the permutation of signs, the inversion of their value and exchanges performed according to the rules of symbolic logic, will, like the philosopher's stone, uncover the deep structure of Being.

The blind Cupid of desire, the emblem of Elizabethan brothels, unveiled divine mysteries to Ficino and Mirandola. The "things base and vile" signify in this new hermetic code the "botome of Goddes secrettes." "Man," wrote Ficino, "ascends to the higher realms without discarding the lower world, and can descend to the lower world without foresaking the higher."[9]

As an epigraph to *The Interpretation of Dreams*, Freud quotes from the *Aeneid*: "*Flectere si nequeo superos, Acheronta movebo* [If I am unable to bend the gods above, I shall move the Underworld.]" Neoplatonic "topocosmos" reappear in Freud's "superego" and the underworld: the repressed, the unconscious, the id. In *Three Contributions to the Theory of Sex* Freud wrote: "The omnipotence of sex nowhere perhaps shows itself stronger than in this one of her aberrations. The highest and lowest in sexuality are everywhere most intimately connected ('From heaven through the world to hell')."[10]

In the Neoplatonic exchange of signs between heaven, earth, and hell, the celestial Venus is situated above, the Venus of animal sex below the sphere of the intellect. As in a mountain lake whose depths reflect the peaks of nearby mountains, the signs of the "bottom" are the image and the reflection of the "top." *Venus vulgaris*, blind pleasure of sex, animal desire, becomes "a tool of the divine," as Ficino called it, an initiation into mysteries which, as in Paul, "eye hath not seen, nor ear heard." "Love is said by Orpheus," wrote Mirandola, "to be without eyes, because he is above the intellect." Above and at the same time below. For the Neoplatonists the descent to the bottom is also an ascent into heaven. Darkness is only another lighting. Blindness is only another seeing.[11] Quoting Homer, Tiresias, and Paul as examples, Mirandola wrote: "Many who were rapt to the vision of spiritual beauty were by the same cause blinded in their corporeal eyes."[12] To the cave prisoners of Plato's parable, everything seen is but a shadow. Shadows are nothing but misty reflections of true beings and things outside the cave. But the shadow indicates the source of the light. "Shadow," a word frequently used by Shakespeare, has many meanings, including "double" and "actor." Oberon, in *A Midsummer Night's Dream*, is called the "king of shadows," and Theseus says of theater: "The best in this kind are but shadows" (5.1.210). Theater is a shadow, that is, a double. "Revelry" also means "revelation." In the Neoplatonic code the "revels" and plays performed by the actor-shadows are, like dreams, texts with a latent content.

And it may be said therefore that the mind has two powers.
. . . The one is the vision of the sober mind, the other is the
mind in a state of love: for when it loses its reason by becoming
drunk with nectar, then it enters into a state of love, diffusing
itself wholly into delight: and it is better for it thus to rage
than to remain aloof from that drunkenness.

This paraphrased translation by Ficino from the *Enneads*
of Plotinus could also be read as a Neoplatonic interpretation
of Apuleius' *Metamorphoses*. In his famous commentary on
the second Renaissance edition of *The Golden Ass* in 1600,
Beroaldus quotes amply from Plato, Proclus, and Origen and
sees in Apuleius' *Metamorphoses* the covert story and the mystical initiation into the secrets of divine love: "For Plato writes
in the *Symposium* that the eyes of the mind begin to see clearly
when the eyes of the body begin to fail."[13]

This commentary might surprise a reader not familiar
with the Neoplatonic exchange of signs, who reads in a
straightforward way the crude story of Lucius transformed
into an ass. His mistress, a maid in a witch's house, confused
magic ointments and transformed him into a quadruped instead of a bird. Beaten, kicked, and starved by his successive
owners, he wanders in his new shape through Thessaly all
the way to Corinth. He witnesses kidnappings, murders, and
rapes; sits with bandits in their cave; attends the blasphemous
rituals of sodomites and eunuch priests, and nearly dies of
exhaustion harnessed with slaves in a mill-house.

The *Satyricon* and *The Golden Ass* use the device of fictional
autobiography. Each successive episode, like the picaresque
novella later, yields a dry picture of human cruelty, lust for
power, and untamed sex. Transformed into a thinking animal, Lucius wanders among unthinking men-animals. The
most revealing episode is the meeting between Lucius, who
performs tricks as a trained donkey in the circus, and the
new Pasiphaë, a wealthy Corinthian matron who, like Titania
under the influence of the love potion, has a specific urge
for animal sex: "Thou art he whom I love, thou art he whom
I onely desire."

The infatuation of lunar Titania with a "sweet bully Bottom" ("So is mine eye enthralled to thy shape" [3.1.134]) is

written under the spell of Apuleius: "how I should with my huge and great legs embrace so faire a Matron, or how I should touch her fine, dainty and silke skinne with my hard hoofes, or how it was possible to kisse her soft, her pretty and ruddy lips, with my monstrous great mouth and stony teeth, or how she, who was so young and tender, could be able to receive me."[14]

Lucius is fearful that his monstrous endowment might "hurt the woman by any kind of meane," but the Greek Titania hastens to dispel his fears: "I hold thee my cunny, I hold thee my nops, my sparrow, and therewithal she eftsoones embraced my body round about." Even the grotesque humor of this strange mating was repeated in *Midsummer Night's Dream:*

> Come, sit thee down upon this flowery bed,
> While I thy amiable cheeks to coy,
> And stick musk-roses in thy sleek smooth head,
> And kiss thy fair large ears, my gentle joy.
> (4.1.1–4)

But *The Golden Ass* contains yet another story inserted into the realistic train of Lucius' adventures in the ass's shape. The love story of Cupid and Psyche, an *anilibus fabula,* or "pleasant old wives' tale," as Adlington calls it, may be the oldest literary version of the fable of "Beauty and the Beast."[15] The fable is known in folk traditions of many nations and distant cultures; catalogs of folk motifs place it in Scandinavia and Sicily, in Portugal and Russia. It also appears in India. In all versions of the fable, a young maiden who is to marry a prince is forbidden to look at her husband at night. In the daytime, he is a beautiful youth. At night she is happy with him, but never sees him and is anxious to know with whom she is sleeping. When she lights the lamp in the bedroom, the lover turns out to be an animal; a white wolf, a bear, an ass in one Hindu version, and most often a monstrous snake. When the wife breaks the night-rule, the husband/night animal departs or dies. In *The Golden Ass* this tale is told by "the trifling and drunken woman" to a virgin named Charite, abducted on the eve of her wedding and threatened with being sold to a brothel. This shocking, realistic frame for the mythical tale of Cupid and Psyche is a true introduction for the testing of *caritas* by *cupiditas,* or of the "top" by the "bottom," in *Metamorphoses.*

Venus herself was jealous of the princess Psyche, the most beautiful of all mortals. She sent out her own son, winged Cupid, to humiliate Psyche and with one of his "piercing darts" to make her fall madly in love "with the most miserablest creature living, the most poore, the most crooked and the most vile, that there may be none found in all the world of like wretchedness." Afterward, like Shakespeare's Titania, she would "wake when some vile thing is near" (2.2.33). But Cupid himself fell in love with Psyche and married her under the condition that she would never cast her eyes upon him in bed. Psyche broke her vow and lit a lamp. A drop of hot oil sputtered from the lamp and Cupid, burnt, ran off forever.

The story of Psyche ends with her giving birth to a daughter called Voluptas. The story of Lucius ends with his resumption of human form and his initiation into the mysteries of Isis and, after the return to Rome, into the rites of Osiris. Initiations are costly, but Lucius, a lawyer in the *collegium* established by Sulla, is able to pay the price of secret rites. The story of Psyche, the most beautiful of all mortal maidens, leads from beauty through the tortures of love to eternal pleasure. The story of Lucius, always sexually fascinated by hair before his own transformation into a hairy ass, leads from earthy delights to humiliating baldness: he is ordered twice to shave his head, once as a high priest of Isis and once for the rites of Osiris.

For Bakhtin, the tradition of *serio ludere* starts with Petronius and Apuleius. But which of the two metamorphoses in *The Golden Ass* is serious and mystical, and in which does one hear only the mocking *risus?*

For Beroaldus, *Metamorphoses* is a Platonic message of transcendent love, written in a cryptic language on two levels above and below reason. From Boccaccio's *Genealogia Deorum* (1472) to Calderón's *auto sacramental,* where the story of Psyche and Amor symbolizes the mystical union of the Church and Christ and ends with the glorification of the Eucharist,

Apuleius was often read as an orphic, Platonic, or Christian allegory of mystical rapture or divine fury. But for at least three centuries *The Golden Ass* was also read in the code of "serious laughter." In *Decameron*, two novellae were adopted from Apuleius. In *Don Quixote*, the episode of the charge on the jugs of wine was repeated after *Metamorphoses*. Adaptations are innumerable: from Molière's *Psychè*, La Fontaine's *Les Amours du Psychè et Cupide*, Le Sage's *Gil Blas*, to Anatole France's *La Rôtisserie de la Reine Pedauque*.[16]

In both the intellectual traditions and the codes of interpretation there are exchanges of icons and signs between the "top" and "bottom," the above and below reason. In the "Platonic translation," where the "above" *logos* outside the cave is the sole truth and the "below" is merely a murky shadow, the signs of the top are the ultimate test of the signs of the bottom. *Venus vulgaris* is but a reflection and a presentiment of the Celestial Venus. In *serio ludere* the top is only *mythos;* the bottom is the human condition. The signs and emblems of the bottom are the earthly probation of the signs and emblems of the top. *Venus celestis* is merely a projection, a mythical image of *amore bestiale*—the untamed libido. The true Olympus is the Hades of Lucian's *Dialogues of the Dead* or of Aristophanes' *Frogs*, where the coward and buffoon Dionysus appears in the cloak of Hercules. Having its origins in Saturnalia, *serio ludere* is a festive *parodia sacra*.

In hermetic interpretations, the story of Psyche and Cupid is a mythic version of Lucius' metamorphosis. The transformation into a donkey is a covert story whose mystical sense is concealed. Within the "carnival" as a code, ritual and poetry, Lucius' adventures in an ass's skin form an overt story concealing the hidden mockery in the tale of Amor and Cupid.

Psyche's two sisters, jealous of her happy marriage, insinuate to her that she shared her bed with a snake and monster. The poor woman does not know what she is really feeling since "at least *in one person* she hateth the beast (*bestiam*) and loveth her husband." As in dreams, the latent content of the story of Psyche and Cupid becomes manifest in Lucius' adventures. The signs of the top are an inversion and a displacement of the signs of the bottom. Like the Corinthian

matron fascinated by "monstrosity," and like Titania aroused
by Bottom's "beastliness," Psyche loved the beast and hated
the husband "in one person." The evil sisters, like a Freudian
analyst, uncovered her deep secret: "this servile and dangerous pleasure [*clandestinae Veneris faetidi periculesique con-
cubitus*] . . . do more delight thee."

In the Neoplatonic metaphysics as well as in the *serio ludere*
of the carnival, the microcosm represents and repeats the
macrocosm, and man is the image of the universe. In the
vertical imagery man is divided in half: from the waist up he
represents the heavens, from the waist down hell. But all
hells, from the antique Tartarus through the hells of Dante
and Hieronymus Bosch, are the image of Earth.

> Down from the waist they are Centaurs,
> Though woman all above:
> But to the girdle do the Gods inherit,
> Beneath is all the fiend's:
> There's hell, there's darkness.
> (*King Lear* 4.6.123–30)

In both systems the signs of the above and the below, the
macro and the micro, correspond to each other and are interchangeable. But their values are opposed both in the Neoplatonic code and in the carnival tradition and, to a certain
extent, in the poetics of tragedy and comedy. From the Saturnalia through the medieval and Renaissance carnivals and
celebrations, the elevated and noble attributes of the human
mind are exchanged—as Bakhtin shows convincingly—for
the bodily functions (with a particular emphasis on the "lower
stratum": defecation, urination, copulation, and childbirth).
In carnival wisdom they are the essence of life: a guarantee
of its continuity.

Titania, like Psyche, was punished. The punishment is
infatuation with the most "base and vile" of human beings.
But this vile and base person is not transformed Cupid but
the Bacchic donkey. Like the Corinthian matron of Apuleius,
Titania sleeps with this carnival ass. In Shakespeare's adaptation of *The Golden Ass*, Psyche and the lascivious Corinthian
matron are combined into the one person of Titania. In *serio*

ludere piety and reverence do not exist as separate from mockery. Seriousness is mockery and mockery is seriousness.

The exchange of signs in *serio ludere* is the very same translation into the bottom, the low, and the obscene that takes place in folk rituals and carnival processions.[17] The masterpiece of carnivalesque literature is Rabelais' *Gargantua and Pantagruel.* In the sixth chapter of the first book, Gargamelle feels birth pangs:

> A few moments later, she began to groan, lament and cry out. Suddenly crowds of midwives came rushing in from all directions. Feeling and groping her below, they found certain loose shreds of skin, of rather unsavory odor, which they took to be a child. It was, on the contrary, her fundament which had escaped with the mollification of her right intestine (you call it the bumgut) because she had eaten too much tripe.[18]

Gargantua's mother had gorged herself so much the previous evening that the child found its natural exit blocked in this carnival physiology.

> As a result of Gargamelle's discomfort, the cotyledons of the placenta of her matrix were enlarged. The child, leaping through the breach and entering the hollow vein, ascended through her diaphragm to a point above her shoulders. Here the vein divides into two: the child accordingly worked his way in a sinistral direction, to issue, finally, through the left ear.

In medieval moral treatises and sermons, the mystery of the virgin birth was explained again and again as the Holy Ghost entering the Virgin through her ear—invariably, through her left ear. The Holy Ghost descended to the Virgin Mary from the top to the bottom so she could conceive immaculately. A blow from the anus in Rabelais' *parodia sacra* propelled Gargantua from the bottom to the top so the child of carnival could be born in the upside-down world.[19] In this bottom translation, earthly *pneuma* replaced the divine one and the movement along the vertical axis of the body, and of the cosmos as well, was reversed. Rabelais appeals directly to Corinthians. The patron saint of this carnival birth was Paul.

> Now I suspect that you do not thoroughly believe this strange nativity. If you do not, I care but little, though an honest and

sensible man believes what he is told and what he finds written. Does not Solomon say in *Proverbs* (14:15): *Innocens credit omni verbo,* the innocent believeth every word, and does not St. Paul (1 Corinthians 13) declare: *Charitas omnia credit,* Charity believeth all?[20]

In carnivalesque literature, the first letter to the Corinthians is quoted as often as in the writings of the Neoplatonists. And the choice of the most favored quotes is nearly the same:

Where *is* the wise? where *is* the scribe? where *is* the disputer of this world? hath not God made foolish the wisdom of the world? (1.20)

And base things of the world, and things which are despised, hath God chosen, *yea*, and things which are not, to bring to naught things that are. (1.28)

If any among you seemeth to be wise in this world, let him become a fool, that he may be wise. For the wisdom of this world is foolishness with God. (3.18–19)

For Florentine Neoplatonists, Paul is the teacher of *supra intellectum* mysteries. But in the carnival rites, the fool is wise and his madness is the wisdom of this world.[21] For Rabelais, and perhaps even more so for Erasmus, the letter to the Corinthians was the praise of folly: "Therefore *Salomon* beyng so great a kynge, was naught ashamed of my name when he saied in his XXX chapitre, '*I am most foole of all men:*' Nor *Paule doctour of the gentiles* . . . when writing to the Corinthians he said: '*I speake it as vnvise, hat I more than others, etc.,*' as who saieth it were a great dishonour for him to be ouercome in folie" (109.29 f.). In Erasmus' *Moriae encomium* Folly speaks in the first person and in its own name. In this most Menippean of Renaissance treatises, Folly appeals to Paul's "foolishness of God" on nearly every page. Near the end of *The Praise of Folly,* Erasmus describes heavenly raptures which, rarely occurring to mortals, may give the foretaste or "savour of that hieghest rewarde" and which, as in Paul, "was neuer mans eie sawe, nor eare heard." But Erasmus' Folly, ever cynical and joyful, is more interested in returning to earth and awakening than in mystical raptures.

> Who se euer therefore haue suche grace . . . by theyr life tyme
> to tast of this saied felicitee, they are subjecte to a certaine
> passion muche lyke vnto madnesse . . . or beyng in a truance,
> thei doo speake certaine thynges not hangyng one with an
> other . . . and sodeinely without any apparent cause why, dooe
> chaunge the state of theyr countenaunces. For now shall ye
> see theim of glad chere, now of as sadde againe, now thei
> wepe, now thei laugh, now thei sighe, for briefe, it is certaine,
> 192that they are wholly distraught and rapte out of theim
> selues. (128.4 ff.)

Bottom speaks much as Folly after awakening from his own dream:

> Man is but an ass, if he go about to expound his dream.
> Methought I was—there is no man can tell what. Methought
> I was—and methought I had—but man is but a patched fool
> if he will offer to say what methought I had. (4.1.205–9)

We may now once more evoke the striking and ambivalent image of the return to daybreak after the mystical orgasm in *The Praise of Folly*.

> In sort, that whan a little after thei come againe to their former
> wittes, thei denie plainly thei wote where thei became, or
> whether thei were than in theyr bodies, or out of theyr bodies,
> wakyng or slepyng: remembring also as little, either what they
> heard, saw, saied, or did than, sauyng as it were through a
> cloude, or by a dreame: but this they know certainely, that
> whiles their mindes so roued and wandred, thei were most
> happie and blisfull, so that they lament and wepe at theyr
> retourne vnto theyr former senses. (128.16 ff.)

Let us now hear once more Bottom speak to his fellows:

> BOTTOM: Masters, I am to discourse wonders: but ask me not
>   what; for if I tell you, I am not a true Athenian. I will tell
>   you every thing, right as it fell out.
> QUINCE: Let us hear, sweet Bottom.
> BOTTOM: Not a word of me.

The Praise of Folly, dedicated to Thomas More, was published in London in Chaloner's translation in 1549 and reprinted twice (1560, 1577), the last time almost twenty years before *A Midsummer Night's Dream*. It is hard to conceive that Shakespeare had never read one of the most provocative books of

the century.[22] Bottom's misquote from Corinthians appears
after his sudden awakening after the stay in "heaven." But
what kind of heaven, the sexual climax in animal shape or
mythical rapture? Apuleius, Paul, and Erasmus meet in Bottom's monologue. Of all encounters in A Midsummer Night's
Dream, this one is least expected. "I have had a most rare
vision. I have had a dream." The same word "vision(s)" was
already uttered by Titania in a preceding scene, upon her
waking from a "dream": "My Oberon, what visions have I
seen!/Methought I was enamour'd of an ass" (4.1.75–76).

III

From Saturnalia to medieval ludi the ass is one of the main
actors in processions, comic rituals, and holiday revels. In
Bakhtin's succinct formula the ass is "the Gospel—symbol of
debasement and humility (as well as concomitant regenera-
tion)." On festive days such as the Twelfth Night, Plough
Monday, the Feast of Fools, and the Feast of the Ass, merry
and often vulgar parodies of liturgy were allowed. On those
days devoted to general folly, clerics often participated as
masters of ceremony, and an "Asinine Mass" was the main
event. An ass was occasionally brought into the church, and
a hymn especially composed for the occasion would be sung:

> Orientis partibus
> Adventavit Asinus
> Pulcher et fortissimus
> Sarcinis aptissimus.

The symbolism of the carnival ass and sacred drôlerie survived from the Middle Ages until Elizabethan times.[23] At the
beginning of Elizabeth's reign donkeys dressed up as bishops
or dogs with Hosts in their teeth would appear in court masques. But more significant than these animal disguises, which
were a mockery of Catholic liturgy, was the appearance of
the Bacchic donkey onstage. In Nashe's Summer's Last Will
and Testament, performed in Croyden in 1592 or 1593, a few
years before A Midsummer Night's Dream, Bacchus rode onto
the stage atop an ass adorned with ivy and garlands of grapes.
    Among all festival masques of animals the figure of the
ass is most polysemic. The icon of an ass, for Bakhtin "the

most ancient and lasting symbol of the material bodily lower stratum," is the ritualistic and carnivalesque mediator between heaven and earth, which transforms the "top" into the earthly "bottom." In its symbolic function of translation from the high to the low, the ass appears both in ancient tradition, in Apuleius, and in the Old and New Testaments as Balaam's she-ass, and as the ass on which Jesus rode into Jerusalem for the last time. "Tell ye the daughter of Si-on, Behold thy King cometh unto thee, meek, and sitting upon an ass, and a colt foal of an ass" (Matt. 21:5). Graffiti from the third century on the wall of the Palace of Caesars on the Palatine in Rome represent Jesus on the cross with an ass's head. In the oldest mystic tradition an ass is a musician who has the knowledge of the divine rhythm and revelation. An ass appears in the medieval *Processus prophetarum* and speaks with a human voice to give testimony to the truth in French and English mystery plays.[24] In Agrippa's *De vanitate scientiarum* (1526) we find the extravagant and striking "The Praise of an Ass" (*Encomium asinu*), which is a succinct repetition of and analogue to Erasmus' *Encomium moriae.*

The bodily meets with the spiritual in the *figura* and the masque of the ass. That is why the mating of Bottom and the Queen of the Fairies, which culminates the night and forest revelry, is so ambivalent and rich in meanings. In traditional interpretations of *A Midsummer Night's Dream,* the personae of the comedy belong to three different "worlds": the court of Theseus and Hippolyta; the "Athenian" mechanicals; and the "supernatural" world of Oberon, Titania, and the fairies. But particularly in this traditional interpretation, the night Titania spent with an ass in her "consecrated bower" must appear all the stranger and more unexpected.

Titania is the night double of Hippolyta, her dramatic and theatrical paradigm. Perhaps, since during the Elizabethan period the doubling of roles was very common, these two parts were performed by the same young boy. This Elizabethan convention was taken up by Peter Brook in his famous production. But even if performed by different actors, Hippolyta's metamorphosis into Titania and her return to the previous state, like Theseus' transformation into Oberon, must have seemed much more obvious and natural to Elizabethan patrons than to audiences brought up on conventions of the fake realism of nineteenth-century theater. A play on the marriage of the Duke of Athens with the Queen of the Amazons was most likely performed at an aristocratic wedding where courtly spectators knew the mythological emblems as well as the rules of a masque.

Court masques during the Tudor and Elizabethan period were composed of three sequels: (1) appearance in mythological or shepherds' costumes; (2) dancing, occasionally with recitation or song; and (3) the ending of the masque, during which the masquers invited the courtly audience to participate in a general dance. Professional actors did not take part in masques, which were courtly masquerades and social entertainment. "Going off" or "taking out," as this last dance was called, ended the metamorphosis and was a return of the masquers to their places at court.

The disguises corresponded to social distinctions. The hierarchies were preserved. Dukes and lords would never consent to represent anyone below the mythological standing of Theseus. Theseus himself could only assume the shape of the "King of the Fairies" and Hippolyta that of the "Queen of the Fairies." The annual Records at the Office of the Revels document the figures that appeared in court masques. Among fifteen sets of masking garments in 1555, there were "Venetian senators," "Venuses," "Huntresses," and "Nymphs." During the Jacobean period Nymphs of English rivers were added to the Amazons and Nymphs accompanying Diana, and Oberon with his knights was added to Actaeon and his hunters. In 1611, nearly fifteen years after A Midsummer Night's Dream, young Henry, the king's son, appeared in the costume of the "faery Prince" in Jonson's Oberon.[25]

The most frequently portrayed and popular figure of both courtly and wedding masque was Cupid. In a painting of the wedding masque of Henry Unton in 1572, the guests seated at a table watch a procession of ten Cupids (five white and five black) acompanied by Mercury, Diana, and her six nymphs.[26] From the early Tudor masque to the sophisticated spectacles at the Jacobean court, Cupid appears with golden wings, in the same attire, and with the same accessories: "a small boye to be cladd in a canvas hose and doblett sylverd over with a payre of winges of gold with bow and aroves, his eyes binded."[27] This Cupid—with or without a blindfold— would randomly shoot his arrows at shepherdesses, sometimes missing:

> But I might see young Cupid's fiery shaft
> Quenched in the chaste beams of the watery moon;
> And the imperial votaress passed on.
>
> (2.1.161–63)

But the Renaissance Cupid, who appears eight times in the poetic discourse of *A Midsummer Night's Dream*, has a different name, a different costume, and a different language as a person onstage. The blindfolded Cupid is "Anglicised" or "translated" into Puck, or Robin Goodfellow. On the oldest woodcut representing the folk Robin Goodfellow, in the 1628 story of his "Mad Pranks and Merry Jests," he holds in his right hand a large phallic candle and in his left hand a large broom. He has goat horns on his head and a goat's cloven feet. He is wearing only a skirt made of animal skins and is accompanied by black figures of men and women dressed in contemporary garments and dancing in a circle. This "folk" Robin Goodfellow is an Anglicized metamorphosis of a Satyr dancing with Nymphs.

This oldest image of Robin Goodfellow might refresh the imagination of scenographers and directors of *A Midsummer Night's Dream* who still see Puck as a romantic elf. But this engraving is equally important for the interpretation of the play, in which Shakespeare's syncretism mixes mythological icons of court masques with the pranks and rites of carnival. In *A Midsummer Night's Dream* the love potion replaces the mythological arrow. In poetic discourse this love potion still comes from the flower which turns red from Cupid's shaft. Shakespeare might have found the "love juice" in Montemayor's pastoral *Diana,* but he transposed the conventional simile into a sharp and evocative gesture, a metaphor enacted onstage: Puck's squeezing the juice from the pansy onto the eyelids of the sleeping lovers.

"And maidens call it 'love-in-idleness' " (2.1.168). The pansy's other folk names are "Fancy," "Kiss me," "Cull me" or "Cuddle me to you," "Tickle my fancy," "Kiss me ere I arise," "Kiss me at the garden gate," and "Pink of my John."[28] These are "bottom translations" of Cupid's shaft.

But in the discourse of *A Midsummer Night's Dream* there is not one flower, but two: "love-in-idleness" and its antidote. The opposition of "blind Cupid" and of Cupid with an "incorporeal eye" is translated into the opposition of mythic flowers: "Diana's bud o'er Cupid's flower/Hath ever such force and blessed power" (4.1.72–73).

The Neoplatonic unity of Love and Chastity is personified in the transformation of Venus into virginal Diana. Neoplatonists borrowed this exchange of signs from a line in Virgil's *Aeneid*, in which Venus appears to Aeneas, carrying "on her shoulder a bow as a huntress would" (1.327). In the semantics of emblems, the bow, as the weapon both of Cupid-love and of Amazon-virgo, was a mediation between Venus and Diana. The harmony of the bow, as Plato called it, was for Pico "harmony in discord," a unity of opposites.[29] From the union of Cupid and Psyche, brutally interrupted on earth, the daughter Voluptas was born in the heavens; from the adulterous relation of Mars and Venus, the daughter Harmony was born. Harmony, as Neoplatonists repeated after Ovid, Horace, and Plutarch, is *concordia discors* and *discordia concors*.

For Elizabethan poets and for carpenters who designed court masques and entertainments, this exchange of icons and emblems became unexpectedly useful in the cult of the Virgin Queen. The transformation of Venus into Diana allowed them to praise Elizabeth simultaneously under the names of Cynthia/Diana and Venus, the goddess of love. In Paris's judgment, as Giordano Bruno explicated in *Eroici furori*, the apple awarded to the most beautiful goddess was symbolically given to the other two goddesses as well: "for in the simplicity of divine essence . . . all these perfections are equal because they are infinite."[30]

George Peele must have read Bruno. In his *Arraignement of Paris*, the first extant English pastoral play with songs and dances by nymphs and shepherdesses, Paris hands the golden prize to Venus.[31] Offended, Diana appeals to the gods on Olympus; the golden orb is finally delivered to Elizabeth, "queen of Second Troy." The nymph Elise is "Queen Juno's peer" and "Minerva's mate": "As fair and lovely as the Queen of Love/As chaste as Dian in her chaste desires" (5.1.86–87).

In Ovid's *Metamorphoses*, "Titania" is one of Diana's names. The bow is an emblem of the Queen of Amazons. In the first scene of act 1, Hippolyta in her first lines evokes the image of a bow: "And then the moon, like to a silver bow/New bent in Heaven, shall behold the night/Of our solemnities" (1.1.9–11). Liturgical carnival starts with the new moon after the winter solstice. The new moon resembles a strung bow. The moon, the "governess of floods" (2.1.103), is a sign of Titania; her nocturnal sports are "moonlight revels" (2.1.141). In the poetical discourse the bow of the Amazons and the bow of the moon relate Hippolyta and Titania.

A sophisticated game of the court, with allegorical eulogies and allusions, is played through the exchange of classical emblems called "hieroglyphiches" by Ben Jonson. Greek Arcadia was slowly moving from Italy to England. Mythical figures and classical themes in masques, entertainments, and plays easily lent themselves to pastoral settings. But in this new pastoral mode the "Queen of the Fairies" was still an allegory of Elizabeth. For the Entertainment of Elvetham behind the palace at the base of wooded hills, an artificial pond in the shape of a half-moon had been constructed. On an islet in the middle, the fairies dance with their queen, singing a song to the music of a consort:

> *Elisa* is the fairest Queene
> That euer trod vpon this greene . . .
> O blessed bee each day and houre,
> Where sweete *Elisa* builds her bowre.

The queen of the fairies, with a garland as an imperial crown, recites in blank verse:

> I that abide in places under-ground
> Aureola, the Queene of Fairy Land
> . . . salute you with this chaplet,
> Giuen me by Auberon, the fairy King.

The Entertainment at Elvetham took place in the autumn of 1591, only a few years before even the latest possible date of *A Midsummer Night's Dream*. Even if Shakespeare had not attended it, this magnificent event was prepared by poets, artists, and musicians with whom he was acquainted. The quarto with the libretto, the lyrics, and the songs of the four-day spectacle in Elizabeth's honor was published and twice reprinted.[32] Oberon, Titania, and the fairies entered the Shakespearean comedy not from old romances such as *Huon of Bordeaux*, but from the stage, perhaps from Greene's play *James IV* in which Oberon dances with the fairies, and most certainly from that masque.

In masques and court pastorals, among the mythological figures next to Cupid we always find Mercury. In *A Midsummer Night's Dream* the place usually assigned to the messenger of the gods is empty. But Mercury is not merely the messenger, the *psychopompos* who induces and interrupts sleep as Puck and Ariel do.[33] Hermes-Mercury belongs to the family of tricksters. The trickster is the most invariable, universal, and constant mythic character in the folklore of all peoples. As a mediator between gods and men—the bottom and the top— the trickster is a special broker: he both deceives the gods and cheats men. The trickster is the personification of mobility and changeability and transcends all boundaries, over-throwing all hierarchies. He turns everything upside-down. Within this world gone mad a new order emerges from chaos, and life's continuity is renewed.[34]

> Jack shall have Jill,
> Nought shall go ill;
> The man shall have his mare again, and all shall be well.
> (3.2.461–63)

In the marvelous syncretism of *A Midsummer Night's Dream*, Puck the trickster is a bottom and carnivalesque translation of Cupid and Mercury.[35] The Harlequin, Fool, and Lord of Misrule—called in Scotland the Abbot of Unreason—belong to this theatrical family of tricksters. The Lord of Misrule was the medieval successor of the *Rex* of the Saturnalia. Puck's practical joke ("An ass's noll I fixed on his head" [3.2.17]) has its origin in the oldest tradition of folk festivities. In the Feast of Fools, or *festum asinorum,* the low clerics parodied the Holy Offices while disguising themselves with the masks of animals.[36] Mummery, painting the face red or white or covering it with grotesque or animal masks, is still often seen during Twelfth Night, Ash Wednesday, or Valentine's Day.

But putting on an ass's head was not only a theatrical repetition of mockeries and jokes of the Feast of Fools or the day of Boy-Bishop. Another universal rite is also repeated when a "boore," a thing "base and vile," or a mock-king of the carnival was crowned, and after his short reign, uncrowned, thrashed, mocked, and abused. As the drunken Christopher Sly, a tinker, is led into the palace in *The Taming of the Shrew,* so the bully Bottom is introduced into Titania's court of fairies. A coronet of flowers winds about his hairy temples, and the queen's servants fulfill all his fancies. Among Bottom's colleagues is also another "Athenian" tinker, Tom Snout. Like Christopher Sly and all mock-kings abused and uncrowned, Bottom, a weaver, wakes from his dream having played only the part of an ass at the court entertainment.

No one created Shakespearean scenes as strange and uncanny as those of Fuseli. "Fuseli's Shakespearean characters," wrote Mario Praz in *Il patto col serpente,* "stretch themselves, arch and contort, human catapults about to burst through the walls of the narrow and suffocating world, oppressed by the pall of darkness on which speaks Lady Macbeth . . . It is a demonic world of obsessions, a museum filled with statues of athletes galvanised into action, galloping furies, falling down onto prostrate corpses in yawning sepulchres."[37] But this demonic world of Shakespeare was recreated by Fuseli not only in his drawings and paintings of *Macbeth, Lear,* and *Richard III:* fear and trembling, rebellion and frenzy are also present in Fuseli's scenes from *A Midsummer Night's Dream.*

The famous Fuseli painting *Titania caressing Bottom with an ass's head* was executed three months after the siege of the Bastille. Titania in a frenetic dance assumes the pose of Leonardo's *Leda.* With only a small transparent sash around her left hip and covering her pudenda, she is almost nude, but her hair is carefully coiffed. She sees no one, her eyes are half closed. The fairies, Pease blossom, Cobweb, Moth, and

Mustardseed, are not from fairyland, but from a rococo party at Court, or from some bizarre masquerade with dwarfs and midgets. At least two fairies wear long robes of white mousseline with decolleté necklines and the English hats seen in the vignettes of Pamela and Grandisson.

Next to Titania sits the huge Bottom, hunched over. He is pensive and sad. He looks as though, by some strange and unpredictable turn of events, he has found himself at a feast whose sense he does not grasp. In another painting by Fuseli, from 1793–94, Bottom looks even more alienated. Titania, naked from the waist up, embraces him lasciviously, and Pease blossom, once again with a hat à la mode, scratches his scalp between his "fair, large ears." But Bottom, with the enormous legs of a rustic, does not belong to the orgy of Titania's court. The strangest being in this painting is a small homunculus with the head of an insect and open legs with masculine genitalia. What is the most strange and unexpected in Fuseli's vision is the atmosphere of fear and trembling at the mating of Titania and Bottom as on the last night at Court before the revolution.

This "insolite" syncretism of *A Midsummer Night's Dream,* as seen by Fuseli, was recreated by Rimbaud in one of the most enigmatic of his *Illuminations* under the title *Bottom:*

> Reality being too prickly for my lofty character, I became at my lady's a big blue-gray bird flying up near the moldings of the ceiling and dragging my wings after me in the shadows of the evening.
>
> At the foot of the baldaquino supporting her precious jewels and her physical masterpieces, I was a fat bear with purple gums and thick sorry-looking fur, my eyes of crystal and silver from the consoles.
>
> Evening grew dark like a burning aquarium.
>
> In the morning—a battling June dawn—I ran to the fields, an ass, trumpeting and brandishing my grievance, until the Sabines came from the suburbs to hurl themselves on my chest.[38]

The raped Sabines from the new suburbs throw themselves upon the neck of the lost ass whining and running on the green. All metamorphoses from *The Golden Ass* and *Beauty and the Beast* are evoked in this short poem in prose. It is the most succinct and astonishing "writerly text" of *A Midsummer Night's Dream*. Rimbaud, with rare intuition, discovered both the mystery and the sexuality ("a network with a thousand entrances") of the strange translation of Bottom.

In traditional performances of *A Midsummer Night's Dream*, which present Bottom's night at Titania's court as a romantic ballet, and in the spectacle staged by Peter Brook and many of his followers which emphasizes Titania's sexual fascination with a monstrous phallus (mea culpa!),[39] the carnival ritual of Bottom's adventure is altogether lost. Even Lucius, as a frustrated ass in Apuleius, was amazed at the sexual eagerness of the Corinthian matron who, having "put off all her garments to her naked skinne . . . began to annoint all her body with balme" and caressed him more adeptly than "in the Courtesan schooles." Bottom appreciates being treated as a very important person, but is more interested in the frugal pleasure of eating than in the bodily charms of Titania.

In Bottom's metamorphosis and in his encounters with Titania, not only do high and low, metaphysics and physics, pathos and burlesque, meet, but so do two theatrical traditions: the masque and the court entertainment meet the carnival world turned upside-down.[40] In masques and entertainments, "noble" characters were sometimes accompanied by Barbarians, Wild Men, Fishwives, and Marketwives. At the Entertainment of Elvetham an "ugly" Nereus showed up, frightening the court ladies.[41] But for the first time in both the history of revels and the history of theater, Titania/Diana/the Queen of Fairies sleeps with a donkey in her "flowery bower."[42] This encounter of Titania and Bottom, the ass and the mock-king of the carnival, is the very beginning of modern comedy and one of its glorious opening nights.

IV

A musical interlude accompanies the transition from night to day: "To the winding of horns [within] enter THESEUS, HIPPOLITA, EGEUS, and Train" (stage direction, 4.1.101). In this poetic discourse, the blowing of the hunters' horns, the barking of the hounds, and the echo from the mountains

are translated into a musical opposition in the Platonic tradition of "discord" and "concord." In this opposition between
day and night, not the night but precisely the musical or-
chestration of daybreak is called discord by Theseus and by
Hippolyta. For Theseus this discord marks "the musical con-
fusion/Of hounds and echo in conjunction" (4.1.109–10). "I
never heard," replies Hippolyta, "so musical a discord, such
sweet thunder" (4.1.116–17). Only a few lines further, when
Lysander and Demetrius kneel at Theseus' feet after the end
of "night-rule," the "discord" of the night turns into the new
"concord" of the day: "I know you two are rival enemies./
How comes this gentle concord in the world?" (4.1.142).[43]

Both terms of the opposition, "concord" and "discord,"
are connected by Theseus when Philostrate, his master of
the revels, hands him the brief of an interlude to be presented
by the "Athenian" mechanicals:

> "A tedious brief scene of young Pyramus
> And his love Thisbe; very tragical mirth"?
> Merry and tragical? Tedious and brief?
> That is hot ice and wondrous strange snow!
> How shall we find the concord of this discord?
> (5.1.56–60)

This new *concordia discors* is a tragicomedy, and good Peter
Quince gives a perfect definition of it when he tells the title
of the play to his actors: "Marry, our play is 'The most lamentable comedy, and most cruel death of Pyramus and
Thisbe' "(1.2.11–12). Although merely an Athenian carpenter, as it turns out, Quince is quite well-read in English rep-
ertory, having styled the title of his play after the "new tragical
comedy" *Damon and Pithias* by Edwards (1565), or after Pres-
ton's *Cambises* (published ca. 1570), a "lamentable comedy
mixed full of pleasant mirth."[44] The same traditional titles,
judged by printers to be attractive to readers and spectators,
appeared on playbills and title pages of quartos: *The comicall
History of the Merchant of Venice* or *The most Excellent and lamentable Tragedie of Romeo and Juliet*. The latter title would fit
better the story of Pyramus and Thisbe.

We do not know, and probably will not discover, whether
Romeo and Juliet or *A Midsummer Night's Dream* was written

earlier. History repeats itself twice, "the first time as tragedy, the second as farce." Marx was right: world history and the theater teach us that *opera buffa* repeats the protagonists and situations of *opera seria*. The "most cruel death" of Romeo and Juliet is changed into a comedy, but this comedy is "lamentable." The new tragicomedy, "concord of the discord," is a double translation of tragedy into comedy and of comedy into burlesque. The burlesque and the parody are not only in the dialogue and in the songs; the "lamentable comedy" is played at Theseus' wedding by the clowns.

Burlesque is first the acting and stage business. A wall separates the lovers, and they can only whisper and try to kiss through a "hole," a "cranny," "chink." This scene's crudity is both naive and sordid, as in sophomoric jokes and jests where innocent words possess obscene innuendo. Gestures here are more lewd than words.

The Wall was played by Snout. Bottom, who also meddled in directing, recommended: "Let him hold his fingers thus" (3.1.65–66). But what was this gesture supposed to be? Neither the text nor the stage directions ("Wall stretches out his fingers" [stage direction, 5.1.175]) are clear. In the nineteenth-century stage tradition, the Wall stretched out his fingers while the lovers kissed through the "cranny." In Peter Hall's Royal Shakespeare Company film (1969), the Wall holds in his hands a brick which he puts between his legs. Only then does he make a "cranny" with his thumb and index finger. But it could have been yet another gesture. The "hole," as the letter V made by the middle and index finger, would be horizontal and vertical. As Thomas Clayton argues, Snout in the Elizabethan theater of clowns straddled and stretched out his fingers between his legs wide apart. "And this the cranny is, right and sinister" (5.1.162). Snout, although an "Athenian" tinker, had a touch of Latin or Italian and knew what "sinister" meant.[45]

Romeo could not even touch Juliet when she leaned out the window. The Wall scene ("O kiss me through the hole of this vile wall" [198]) is the "bottom translation" of the balcony scene from *Romeo and Juliet*. The sequel of suicides is the same in both plays. But Thisbe "dies" differently. The burlesque Juliet stabs herself perforce with the scabbard of Pyramus' sword.[46] This is all we know for certain about how *A Midsummer Night's Dream* was performed in Shakespeare's lifetime.

The lovers from Athens did not meet a lion during their nightly adventure as Pyramus and Thisbe did in their forest, nor a dangerous lioness as Oliver and Orlando did in the very similar forest of Arden in *As You Like It*. But the menace of death hovers over the couple from the very beginning: "Either to die the death, or to abjure" (1.1.65). The *furor* of love always calls forth death as its only equal partner. Hermia says to Lysander: "Either death or you I'll find immediately" (2.2.155); Lysander says of Helena: "Whom I do love, and will do till my death" (3.2.167); Helena says of Demetrius: "To die upon the hand I love so well" (2.1.244), and again: "tis partly my own fault./Which death, or absence soon shall remedy" (3.2.243–44). Even sleep "with leaden legs and batty wings" is "death counterfeiting" (3.2.364).

In this polyphony of sexual frenzy, neither the classical Cupid with his "fiery shaft" nor the Neoplatonic Cupid with his "incorporeal eye" is present any longer. Desire ceases to hide under the symbolic cover. Now is the action of the body which seeks another body. In the language of the earthly gravitation, the eye sees the closeness of the other body, and the hand seeks rape or murder. The other is the flesh. But "I" is also the flesh. "My mistress with a monster is in love" (3.2.6).

"Death" and "dead" are uttered twenty-eight times; "dying" and "die" occur fourteen times. The field of "death" appears in nearly fifty verses of *A Midsummer Night's Dream* and is distributed almost evenly among the events in the forest and the play at Theseus' wedding. The frequency of "kill" and "killing" is thirteen, and "sick" and "sickness" occur six times. In *A Midsummer Night's Dream*, which has often been called a happy comedy of love, "kiss" and "kissing" occur only six times, always within the context of the burlesque; "joy" occurs eight times, "happy" six, and "happiness" none.

The forest happenings during the premarital night are only the first sports in *A Midsummer Night's Dream;* the main merriment is provided by clowns. In the "mirths," in the forest and at court, Bottom is the leading actor. While rehearsing his part in the forest, "sweet Pyramus" was "translated" into an ass. He "dies" onstage as Pyramus, only to be called an ass by Theseus: "With the help of a surgeon, he might yet recover, and prove an ass" (5.1.298–300).

If Bottom's metamorphoses in the forest and at court are read synchronically, as one reads an opera score, the "sweet bully" boy in both of his roles—as an ass and as Pyramus—sleeps with the queen of the fairies, is crowned and uncrowned, dies, and is resurrected onstage. The true director of the night-rule in the woods is Puck, the Lord of Misrule. The interlude of Pyramus and Thisbe was chosen for the wedding ceremonies by Philostrate, the master of revels to Theseus. Within *A Midsummer Night's Dream*, performed as an interlude at an aristocratic wedding, the play within a play is a paradigm of comedy as a whole. The larger play has an enveloping structure: the small "box" repeats the larger one, as a wooden Russian doll contains smaller ones.

The change of partners during a single night and the mating with a "monster" on the eve of a marriage of convenience do not appear to be the most appropriate themes for wedding entertainment. Neither is the burlesque suicide of the antique models of Romeo and Juliet the most appropriate merriment for "a feast of great solemnity."[47] All dignity and seriousness vanish from the presentation of the "most cruel death of Pyramus and Thisbe." The night adventure of Titania and two young couples is reduced to a "dream." "And think no more of this night's accidents/But as the fierce vexation of a dream" (4.1.67–68).

"The lunatic, the lover and the poet,/Are of imagination all compact" (5.1.7–8). These lines of Theseus, like those of Helena's monologue from the first scene in act 1, are a part of the poetic metadiscourse whose theme is self-referential: the dreams in *A Midsummer Night's Dream* and the whole play. And as in Helena's soliloquy, Neoplatonic oppositions return in it. Ficino, in *In Platonis Phaedrum* and in *De amore*, distinguishes four forms of inspired madness: *furor divinus*, the "fine frenzy" of the poet; "the ravishment of the diviner";

"the prophetic rapture of the mystic"; and the "ecstasy of the lover," *furor amatorius.*[48]
Even more important than the repetition of Neoplatonic categories of "madness" is the inversion by Theseus/Shakespeare of the values and hierarchy in this exchange of topos:

> The poet's eye, in a fine frenzy rolling,
> Doth glance from heaven to earth, from earth to heaven;
> And as imagination bodies forth
> The forms of things unknown, the poet's pen
> Turns them to shapes, and gives to airy nothing
> A local habitation and a name.
>
> (5.1.12–17)

As opposed to the "fine frenzy" of the Platonic poet, Shakespeare's pen gives earthly names to shadows, "airy nothing," and relocates them on earth.[49] The "lunatic" who "sees more devil than vast hell can hold" (5.1.9) replaces Neoplatonic mystics. The frenzied lover "sees Helen's beauty in a brow of Egypt" (5.1.11). All three—"the lunatic, the lover and the poet"—are similar to a Don Quixote who also gave to "phantasies," shadows of wandering knights, the "local habitation and a name"; who saw a beautiful Dulcinea in a coarse country maid; and, like a Shakespearean madman who in a "bush supposed a bear" (5.1.22), would charge windmills with his lance, taking them to be giants, and stormed wineskins, thinking them to be brigands.

> Lovers and madmen have such seething brains,
> Such shaping phantasies, that apprehend
> More than cool reason ever comprehends.
>
> (5.1.4–6)

In this metadiscourse, which is at the same time self-defeating and self-defending, a manifesto of Shakespeare's dramatic art and a defense of his comedy are contained. "More than cool reason ever comprehends" is not the Platonic "shadow" and the metaphysical *supra intellectum* of Pico and Ficino. "More than cool reason ever comprehends" is, as in Paul, the "foolish things of the world" which God designed "to confound the wise." This "foolishness of God," taken from the Corinthians, read and repeated after the carnival tradition, is the defense of the Fool and the praise of Folly.

The lunatics—the Fool, the Lord of Misrule, the Abbot of Unreason—know well that when a true king, as well as the carnival mock-king, is thrown off, he is turned into a thing "base and vile, holding no quantity"; that there are "more devils than vast hell can hold" and that Dianas, Psyches, and Titanias sleep not with winged Cupids but with an ass. "Bless thee, Bottom, bless thee! Thou art translated." You are translated. But into what language? Into a language of the earth. The bottom translation is the wisdom of Folly and delight of the Fool.

V

Bottom, soon after his death onstage, springs up and bids farewell to Wall with an indecent gesture. Thisbe is also resurrected; her body cannot remain onstage. The merry, joyful, and playful Bergomask ends the clowns' spectacle. It is midnight, and all three pairs of lovers are anxious to go to bed. In a ceremonial procession they leave the stage, illuminated by the torchbearers.

The stage is now empty for a moment. If *A Midsummer Night's Dream* was performed in the evening during the wedding ceremony, the stage was by then cast in shadows. Only after a while does Puck, the Master of night-rule, return to the stage.

> Now the hungry lion roars
> And the wolf behowls the moon . . .
> Now is the time of night
> That the graves, all gaping wide,
> Every one lets forth his sprite
> In the church-way paths to glide.
> (5.1.357–58, 365–68)

The somber line of Puck would be more appropriate for the night when Duncan was murdered than as a solemn "epithalamium" for the wedding night of the noble couple. The "screeching loud" (5.1.362) of the owl and "the triple Hecate's team" (5.1.370) are evoked in Puck's lines, as they were on the night of the regicide in *Macbeth*. It is the same night during which Romeo and Juliet, and Pyramus and Thisbe, committed suicide, during which Hermia might have killed Helena and Demetrius might have killed Lysander.[50]

Hecate is *triformis:* Proserpina in Hades, Diana on earth, and Luna in the heavens, Hecate/Luna/Titania is the mistress of this midnight hour when night starts changing into a new day. But it is still the night during which elves dance "following darkness like a dream" (5.1.372). Wedding follows the evocation of the rite of mourning.

Puck is holding a broom in his hand; the broom was a traditional prop of the rural Robin Goodfellow: "I am sent with broom before/To sweep the dust behind the door" (5.1.375–76). In this sweeping of the floor there is a strange and piercing sadness. Puck sweeps away dust from the stage, as one sweeps a house. Sweeping away recurs in all carnival and spring rituals in England, France, Italy, Germany, and Poland. The symbolism of sweeping is rich and complex. A broom is a polysemic sign. But invariably sweeping away is a symbol of the end and of the beginning of a new cycle. One sweeps rooms away after a death and before a wedding. Goethe beautifully shows this symbolism of sweeping on Saint John's Night:

> Let the children enjoy
> The fires of the night of Saint John,
> Every broom must be worn out,
> And children must be born.

In Eckermann's *Conversations with Goethe,* Goethe quotes his poem and comments: "It is enough for me to look out of the window to see, in the brooms which are used to sweep the streets and in the children running about the streets, the symbols of life ever to be worn out and renewed."[51] Puck's sweeping of the stage with a broom is a sign of death and of a wedding which is a renewal. This is but the first epilogue of *A Midsummer Night's Dream.*

There is yet another. Oberon and Titania, with crowns of waxen tapers on their heads, enter the darkened stage with their train. They sing and dance a pavane. At a court wedding they might have invited the guests to participate in

the dance together: "Every fairy take his gait" (5.1.402). Peter
Brook, in his famous staging, had the house lights come up
while the actors stretched their hands out to the audience
and threw them flowers.

Titania and Oberon appear for the second time in the
play as the night doubles of their day shapes. If they are the
same pair of actors who play Theseus and Hippolyta, Puck's
soliloquy would give them enough time to change their costumes. The enveloping structure of the play had led, with
astounding dramatic logic, to its final conclusion. Theseus
and Titania, Philostrate, Hermia and Helena, Lysander and
Demetrius—the spectators onstage of the "most lamentable
comedy"—are the doubles of the audience watching A Midsummer Night's Dream in the house. The illusion of reality, as
in Northrop Frye's succinct and brilliant formulation, becomes the reality of illusion. "Shadows"—doubles—are actors. But if actors-shadows are the doubles of spectators, the
spectators are the doubles of actors.

> If we shadows have offended,
> Think but this, and all is mended,
> That you have but slumbr'd here,
> While these visions did appear.
>   (5.1.409–12)

Only Puck is left on the stage. This is the third and last
epilogue. "Gentles, do not reprehend" (5.1.415). As in *As You
Like It* and *The Tempest,* the leading actor asks the public to
applaud. But who is Puck in this third and last epilogue?

> The spirit Comus (Revelry), to whom men owe their revelling,
> is stationed at the doors of chamber . . . Yet night is not rep-
> resented as a person, but rather it is suggested by what is
> going on; and the splendid entrance indicated that it is a
> wealthy pair just married who are lying on the couch . . . And
> what else is there of the revel? Well, what but the revellers?
> Do you not hear the castanets and the flute's shrill note and
> the disorderly singing? The torches give a faint light, enough
> for the revellers to see what is close in front of them but not
> enough for us to see them. Peals of laughter arise, and women
> rush along with men, wearing men's sandals and garments
> girt in a strange fashion; for the revel permits women to
> masquerade as men, and men to "put on women's garb" and
> to ape the talk of women. Their crowns are no longer free

but, crushed down to the head on account of the wild running of the dancers, they have lost their joyous look.[52]

This quotation is from Philostratus, the Greek Sophist and scholar (ca. 176–245), whose *Imagines* became, during the Renaissance in Latin translation, one of the most popular textbooks and models for ancient icons of gods and mythical events. The most famous and most frequently quoted chapter of *Imagines* was "Comus." Shakespeare could not have found a more appropriate name for Theseus' Master of the Revels. Philostratus became Philostrate at the "Athenian" court, so that in a system of successive exchanges he would be transformed into Puck, Lord of Misrule, and return in the epilogue to his antique prototype, the god of revelry and the festivities, Comus of the *Imagines* written by Philostratus the Sophist.[53]

There will always remain two interpretations of *A Midsummer Night's Dream:* the light and the somber. And even as we choose the light one, let us not forget the dark one. Heraclitus wrote: "If it were not to Dionysus that they performed the procession and sang the hymn to the pudenda, most shameful things would have been done. Hades and Dionysus are the same, to whichever they rave and revel."[54] In the scene described by Philostratus, Comus is holding a torch downward. He is standing with his legs crossed, in a slumbering stance, at the entrance to the wedding chamber. His pose is that of a funerary Eros of Roman sarcophagi.[55] At the end of *A Midsummer Night's Dream*'s first epilogue, Puck could assume the pose of the funerary Eros. Shakespeare is a legatee of all myths.

In both interpretations of *A Midsummer Night's Dream,* the bottom translation is full of different meanings. All of them, even in their contradiction, are important. The intellectual and dramatic richness of this most striking of Shakespeare's comedies consists in its evocation of the tradition of *serio ludere*. Only within "the concord of this discord" does blind Cupid meet the golden ass and the spiritual become transformed into the physical. The *coincidentia oppositorum* for the first time and most beautifully was presented onstage.

Translated by Daniela Miedzyrzecka

Notes

1.   All quotations from *A Midsummer Night's Dream* are taken from *The Arden Shakespeare*, ed. Harold F. Brooks (London: Methuen, 1979).

2.   *The Praise of Folie*, "A booke made in Latine by that great clerke Erasmus Roterodame. Englisshed by sir Thomas Chaloner knight. Anno 1549." All quotations after Clarence F. Miller ed. (London: Oxford University Press, 1965).

3.   Erwin Panofsky, "Blind Cupid," in *Studies in Iconology: Humanistic Themes in the Art of the Renaissance* (1939; rpt. New York: Harper & Row, 1972), pp. 95–128; Edgar Wind, "Orpheus in Praise of Blind Love," in *Pagan Mysteries in the Renaissance* (New York: Norton, 1968), pp. 53–80.

4.   Frank Kermode, "The Mature Comedies," *Early Shakespeare* (New York: St. Martin's, 1961), pp. 214–20; Paul A. Olsen, "*A Midsummer Night's Dream* and the Meaning of Court Marriage," *ELH* 24 (1957): 95–119.

5.   "The commentary on a single text is not a contingent activity, assigned the reassuring alibi of the 'concrete': the single text is valid for all the texts of literature, not in that it represents them (abstracts and equalizes them), but in that literature itself is never anything but a single text: the one text is not an (inductive) access to a Model, but entrance into a network with a thousand entrances." Roland Barthes, *S/Z*, trans. Richard Miller (New York: Hill & Wang, 1974), p. 12.

6.   *The Xi Bookes of The Golden Asse, Conteininge the Metamorphosie of Lucius Apuleius*. "Translated out of Latine into Englishe by William Adlington. Anno 1566." Rpt. 1571, 1582, 1596. All quotations after Ch. Whibley ed. (London, 1893).

7.   Mikhail Bakhtin, *Problems of Dostoevsky's Poetics*, trans. R. W. Rotsel (Ann Arbor: Ardis, 1973), pp. 88–89.

8.   Claude Lévi-Strauss, *Le Cru et le cuit* (Paris: Plon, 1964), p. 20.

9.   Quoted in Panofsky, "Blind Cupid," p. 137.

10.   *The Basic Writings of Sigmund Freud* (New York: Random House, 1938), p. 572.

11.   "Perhaps good king Oedipus had one eye too many" (Hölderlin, *In Lovely Blueness*).

12.   Wind, "Orpheus," p. 58.

13.   Ibid., pp. 58–59.

14.   Shakespeare's borrowings from *The Golden Ass* in *A Midsummer Night's Dream* (the meeting with the Corinthian lady, and the story of Psyche) were first noted by Sister M. Generosa in "Apuleius and *A Midsummer Night's Dream*: Analogue or Source. Which?" in *Studies in Philology* 42 (1945): 198–204. James A. S. McPeek, "The Psyche Myth and *A Midsummer Night's Dream*," *Shakespeare Quarterly* 23 (1972): 69–79.

15.   Emmanuel Cosquin, *Contes populaires de Lorraine* (Paris: V. F. Vieweg, 1886), 1:xxxii and 2:214–30.

16.   Elizabeth Hazelton Haight, *Apuleius and His Influence* (New York: Cooper Square, 1963), pp. 90 ff.

17.   "The theme of role reversal was commonplace in folk imagery from the end of the Middle Ages through the first half of the nineteenth century:

engravings or pamphlets show, for instance, a man straddling an upside-down donkey and being beaten by his wife. In some pictures mice eat cats. A wolf watches over sheep; they devour him. Children spank parents. . . . Hens mount roosters, roosters lay eggs. The king goes on foot." Emmanuel Le Roy Ladurie, *Carnival in Romans*, trans. M. Finey (New York: Braziller, 1979), p. 191. "Hot ice" and "wondrous strange snow" (5.1.59) belong to this carnival language.

18.   Passages from *Gargantua and Pantagruel* in Jacques Leclerq's translation (New York: Heritage Press, 1964).

19.   From twelfth-century liturgical songs (*Gaude Virgo, mater Christi/Quae per aurem concepisti*) up to Molière's *The School for Wives* ("She came and asked me in a puzzled way . . . if children are begotten through the ear") we have an interrupted tradition, first pious, later parodic, of the virgin conceiving through the ear. See Gaston Hall, "Parody in *L'Ecole des femmes:* Agnès's Question," *MLR* 57 (1962): 63–65. See also Claude Gaignebet, *Le Carnaval* (Paris: Payot, 1974), p. 120.

20.   Rabelais possibly feared that the joke went too far, and this entire passage, beginning with "Does not Solomon" disappeared from the second and subsequent editions of *Gargantua*. Rabelais also ironically quotes from Corinthians in chapter 8, at the end of the description of his medallion with a picture of the hermaphrodite.

21.   "Rabelais' entire approach, his *serio ludere*, the grotesque mask, is deeply justified by his conviction that true wisdom often disguises itself as foolishness. . . . Because he is the most foolish, Panurge receives the divine revelation: the 'Propos des bien yvres,' apparent gibberish, contains God's truth." Florence M. Weinberg, *The Wine and the Will: Rabelais's Bacchic Christianity* (Detroit: Wayne State University Press, 1972), p. 149.

22.   Ronald F. Miller, in *"A Midsummer Night's Dream:* The Fairies, Bottom and the Mystery of Things," *Shakespeare Quarterly*, vol. 26 (1975), pointed out the possibility of a relation between Chaloner's translation and Bottom's monologue. This essay is perhaps the most advanced attempt at an allegorical, almost Neoplatonic interpretation of *A Midsummer Night's Dream;* the "mystery of the fairies" points to "other mysteries in the world offstage" (p. 266).

23.   Mikhail Bakhtin, *Rabelais and His World*, trans. Helene Iswolsky (Cambridge, Mass.: MIT, 1968), pp. 78, 199; Enid Welsford, *The Fool* (London: Faber & Faber, 1935), pp. 200 ff.; E. K. Chambers, *The Medieval Stage* (Oxford: Oxford University Press, 1903), 1:13–15.

24.   Hardin Craig, *English Religious Drama of the Middle Ages* (Oxford: Clarendon, 1960), p. 68; Anderson, pp. 20–21. See also Grace Frank, *The Medieval French Drama* (Oxford: Oxford University Press, 1954, rpt. 1967), pp. 40–42: "At Rouen the play, preserved in several manuscripts, is frankly entitled *Ordo Processionis Asinorum*, although Balaam is only one of the more than twenty-eight characters involved. . . . The ass itself was not necessarily a comic figure; it served as the mount of the Virgin for the Flight into Egypt and of Christ for the Entry into Jerusalem; moreover it was associated with the ox in *praesepe* observances and at all times has been regarded as a faithful, patient beast of burden. But at the feast of the subdeacons the ass undoubtedly became an object of fun, a fact apparent from later church decrees forbidding its presence there."

"Quite probably the appearance of Balaam and his *obstinata bestia* in the prophet play owes something to the revels of the Feast of Fools: though the *Ordo Prophetarum* is the older ceremony, it seems likely that the use of the ass there was introduced late, perhaps as a kind of counter-attraction to the merrymaking of the subdeacons, 'an attempt to turn the established presence of the ass in the church to purposes of edification, rather than ribaldry' (Chambers, ii. 57). In any case the curious title of the Rouen play must be due to the conspicuous figure of Balaam and his *asina*, a beast that seems to have wandered into the prophet play from the Feast of Fools."

25.   E. K. Chambers, *The Elizabethan Stage* (Oxford: Clarendon, 1923), 1:158 ff, 192. According to Chambers, Henry had appeared earlier in Daniel's masque *Twelve Goddesses* (1604), "taken out" and as a child "tost from hand to hand," 1:199.

26.   Chambers, *The Elizabethan Stage*, 1:163–64: The reproduction of a painting on frontispiece in vol. 1.

27.   Letter of George Ferrars, appointed Lord of Misrule by Edward VI. Quoted: Enid Welsford, *The Court Masque* (New York: Russell & Russell, 1927), p. 146.

28.   *A Midsummer Night's Dream*, ed. Henry Cuningham, Arden Shakespeare (London: Methuen, 1905), note to 2.1.168. The poetic name of the love-potion flower was "lunary." In Lyly's *Sapho and Phao:* "an herbe called Lunary, that being bound to the pulses of the sick, causes nothinge but dreames of wedding and daunces" (3.3.43); in *Endymion:* "On yonder banke neuer grove any thing but Lunary, and hereafter I neuer haue any bed but that banke" (2.3.9–10). *The Complete Works of John Lyly*, ed. R. Warwick Bend (Oxford: Clarendon, 1902), 3:38, 508.

29.   The harmony of the string symbolized for the Neoplatonists the *concordia discors* between the passions and the intellect: the bow's arrows wound, but the bowstring itself is held immobile by the hand and guided by the controlling eye. Wind, "Orpheus," pp. 78f, 86f.

30.   Ibid., p. 77.

31.   In *The Arraignement of Paris,* performed at court ca. 1581–84, published in 1584, Venus bribes Paris. In this "Venus show," Helena appears accompanied by four Cupids. The court masque is mixed with pastoral play. Yet perhaps for the first time the "body" of a nymph who fell unhappily in love appears on stage with a "crooked churl"—a folk Fool. But even if Peele's play did not influence Shakespeare, it does nevertheless demonstrate how, at least ten years before *A Midsummer Night's Dream*, Neoplatonic similes of blind and seeing Cupid became a cliché of euphuistic poetry. ("And Cupid's bow is not alone in his triumph, but his rod . . . His shafts keep heaven and earth in awe, and shape rewards for shame" [3.5.33, 36]; "Alas, that ever Love was blind, to shoot so far amiss!" [3.5.7].) Only Shakespeare was able to put new life into these banalities.

32.   The entertainment at Elvetham was prepared by, among others, Lyly, Thomas Morley, the organ player and choirmaster in St. Peters, and the composers John Baldwin and Edward Johnson. Ernest Brennecke, "The Entertainment at Elvetham, 1591," in *Music in English Renaissance Drama* (Lexington: University of Kentucky Press, 1968), pp. 32–172.

33. The *locus classicus* of Hermes, the *psychopompos* who induces and dispels dreams, is in the first lines of the last book of the *Odyssey:* "Meanwhile Cyllenian Hermes was gathering in the souls of the Suitors, armed with the splendid golden wand that he can use at will to cast a spell on our eyes or wake us from the soundest sleep. He roused them up and marshalled them with this, and they obeyed his summons gibbering like bats that squeak and flutter in the depths of some mysterious cave" (*Odyssey*, trans. R. V. Rieu [Baltimore: Penguin, 1946]).

34. "Fundamentally trickster tales represent the way a society defines the boundaries, states its rules and conventions (by showing what happens when the rules are broken), extracts order out of chaos, and reflects on the nature of its own identity, its differentiation from the rest of the universe." Brian V. Street, "The Trickster Theme: Winnebago and Azanda," in *Zandae Themes*, ed. André Singer and Brian V. Street (Oxford: Oxford University Press, 1972), pp. 82–104. "Thus, like Ash-boy and Cinderella, the trickster is a mediator. Since his mediating function occupies a position half-way between two polar terms, he must retain something of that duality—namely an ambiguous and equivocal character." Claude Lévi-Strauss, *Structural Anthropology* (New York: Basic, 1963), p. 226.

35. Puck was originally played by a mature actor, not by a young boy. Only since the Restoration has a ballerina played the part of Puck, as well as Oberon. Peter Brook, in his *Midsummer Night's Dream* (1970), repeated the Elizabethan tradition and had Puck's role performed by a tall and comical actor, John Kane ("thou lob of spirits" [2.1.16]).

36. See Anderson, p. 20.

37. Mario Praz, "Fuseli," in *Il patto col serpente* (Milan: Mondadori, 1972), p. 15. See also T. S. R. Boase, "Illustrations of Shakespeare's Plays in the Seventeenth and Eighteenth Centuries," in *Journal of the Warburg and Courtauld Institutes*, vol. 10 (1947). See also *John Heinrich Fuseli (1741–1825)* (Musée du Petit Palais, 1975.)

38. Rimbaud, *Complete Works*, trans. Wallace Fowlie (Chicago: University of Chicago Press, 1966), p. 227. On the impact of Fuseli on Gautier and on the debt of Rimbaud to Gautier, see Jean Richer, *Etudes et recherches sur Théophile Gautier prosateur* (Paris: Nizet, 1981), pp. 213–23.

39. "In the most solid and dramatic parts of his play [*MND*] Shakespeare is only giving an idealized version of courtly and country revels and of the people that played a part in them." Welsford, *The Court Masque*, p. 332. The most valid interpretation of the festive world in Shakespeare's plays remains still, after over thirty years, C. L. Barber's *Shakespeare's Festive Comedy.*

40. See Jan Kott, "Titania and the Ass's Head," in *Shakespeare Our Contemporary* (New York: Doubleday, 1964), pp. 207–28.

41. On the second day of interrupted spectacles Nereus appeared "so ugly as he ran toward his shelter that he 'affrighted a number of the country people, that they ran from him for feare, and thereby moved great laughter' " (Brennecke, "Entertainment," p. 45). Snout's fears that the ladies will be frightened by a lion are usually considered to be an allusion to the harnessing of a black moor to a chariot instead of a lion during the fes-

tivities of the christening of Prince Henry in 1594; perhaps it is also an amusing echo of "ugly" Nereus who frightened the ladies at Elvetham.

42.   Even in Ben Jonson, who introduced the "anti-Masque," or false masque (in *The Masque of Blackness,*1605), figures of the "anti-Masque" never mix with persons of the masque: they "vanish" after the "spectacle of strangenesse," before the allegories of order and cosmic harmony start. As Jonson emphasized:

> For Dauncing is an exercise
> not only shews ye mouers wit,
> but maketh ye beholder wise
> as he hath powre to rise to it.
> (*Works* [1941], 7:489)

See John C. Meagher, "The Dance and the Masques of Ben Jonson," *Journal of the Warburg and Courtauld Institutes* 25 (1962): 258–77.

43.   For Shakespeare's use of the terms "concord" and "discord" with musical connotations, see: *Richard II,* 5.5.40 ff., *Two Gentlemen of Verona* 1.2.93 ff., *Romeo and Juliet* 3.5.27, *The Rape of Lucrece,* line 1124. See also E. W. Naylor, *Shakespeare and Music* (New York: Da Capo, 1965), p. 24.

44.   Grimald's *Christus Redivivus,* performed in Oxford in 1540 (published in 1543), bears the subtitle "Comoedia Tragica." This is probably the earliest mixture in England of "comedy" and "tragedy" in one term. For the history of titles used by Peter Quince, it is interesting to note *The lamentable historye of the Pryunce Oedipus* (1563) and *The lamentable and true tragedie of M. Arden of Feversham in Kent* (1592). *The tragedy of Pyramus and Thisbe,* published by Geoffrey Bullough (*Narrative and Dramatic Sources of Shakespeare* [London, 1966], 3:411–22) as an "Analogue" to *A Midsummer Night's Dream,* bears the subtitle: "Tragoedia miserrima." Chambers suspects that it is a seventeenth-century product, perhaps by Nathaniel Richards. Bullough holds that it dates from the sixteenth century. Richards' authorship appears to me out of the question; the language and Latin marginalia suggest that this "Tragoedia miserrima" is earlier than *A Midsummer Night's Dream.*

45.   Thomas Clayton, " 'Fie What a Question That If Thou Wert Near a Lewd Interpreter': The Wall Scene in *A Midsummer Night's Dream,*" *Shakespeare Studies* 7 (1974): 101–12; I. W. Robinson, "Palpable Hot Ice: Dramatic Burlesque in *A Midsummer Night's Dream,*" *Studies in Philology* 61 (1964): 192–204.

46.   The last words of Juliet ("O happy dagger,/This is thy sheath; there rest, and let me die") are not the most fortunate, and almost ask for burlesquing.

47.   Three other interludes for wedding entertainments offered by Philostrate seem even less appropriate for the occasion. The strangest one is the first: " 'The battle with the Centaurs, to be sung/By an Athenian eunuch to the harp' " (5.1.44–45). Commentators and notes invariably referred one to Ovid's *Metamorphosis* (12.210 ff.) or else to the "Life of Theseus" in North's *Plutarch.* But the *locus classicus* of this battle with centaurs in the Renaissance tradition was quite different. It is Lucian's *Symposium* or *A Feast of Lapithae,* in which the mythical battle of the Centaurs with the Lapiths is a part of a satirical description of a brawl of philosophers at a contemporary wedding: "The bridegroom . . . was taken off with head in

bandages—in the carriage in which he was to have taken his bride home."
The Works of Lucian of Samosata, trans. H. W. Fowler and F. G. Fowler (Oxford: Oxford University Press, 1905), 4:144. In Apuleius' *The Golden Ass*
unfortunate Charite also evokes the wedding interrupted by Centaurs in
her story of her abduction by bandits from her would-be wedding: "In
this sort was our marriage disturbed, like the marriage of Hypodame."
Rabelais in *Gargantua and Pantagruel* also evokes that unfortunate wedding:
"Do you call this a wedding? . . . Yes, by God, I call it the marriage described
by Lucian in his *Symposium.* You remember; the philosopher of Samosata
tells how the King of the Lapithae celebrates a marriage that ended in war
between Lapithae and Centaurs" (4.15). Shakespeare's ironical intention
in evoking this proverbially interrupted marriage appears self-evident.

48. Panofsky, "Blind Cupid," p. 140; and Kermode, *Shakespeare, Spenser,
Donne* (London: Routledge & Kegan Paul, 1971), p. 209: "To Pico, to
Cornelius Agrippa, to Bruno, who distinguished nine kinds of fruitful
love-blindness, this exaltation of the madness of love was both Christian
and Orphic."

49. Michel Foucault, in *The Order of Things* (1966; New York: Vintage,
1971), discusses in his chapter on *Don Quixote* this new confrontation of
poetry and madness, beginning at the age of Baroque: "But it is no longer
the old Platonic theme of inspired madness. It is the mark of a new experience of language and things. At the fringes of a knowledge that separates beings, signs, and similitudes, and as though to limit its power, the
madman fulfills the function of *homosemanticism:* he groups all signs together and leads them with a resemblance that never ceases to proliferate.
The poet fulfills the opposite function: his is the allegorical role; beneath
the language of signs and beneath the interplay of their precisely delin-
eated distinctions, he strains his ears to catch that 'other language,' the
language, without words or discourse, of resemblance" (pp. 49–50). But
the poet in Theseus' lines is compared to the madman, and his function
is to destroy the "allegorization." The exchange between the noble functions of mind and the low function of body is a radical criticism of all
appearances, and an attempt to show a real similitude of "things" and
"attitudes."

50. Cf. the recitation of "fatal birds" by Bosola to the Duchess of Malfi
in her cell before her strangling: "Hark, now everything is still,/The schreech
owl, and the whistler shrill/Call upon our dame, aloud,/And bid her quickly
don her shroud" (*The Duchess of Malfi* 4.2.179 ff.). An epithalamium, which
bade such creatures to be silent on the wedding night, is astonishingly
similar to the foreboding of the fearful events. In the carnival rites often,
especially in the South, the images of death and wedding meet.

51. *Conversations with Goethe,* January 17, 1827. Quoted by Bakhtin, in
Rabelais, pp. 250–51.

52. Philostratus, *Imagines,* trans. Arthur Fairbanks (London: Heinemann,
1931), pp. 9 ff. Philostratus, a Greek writer (ca. 170–245), author of *The
Life of Apollonius of Tyana* and of *Imagines,* was well known during the
Renaissance. *Opera quae extant* in Greek with Latin translation had been
published in Venice, 1501–4, 1535, 1550, and in Florence in 1517. The
"Stephani Nigri elegatissima" translation had at least three editions (Milan,
1521, 1532; Basel, 1532). *Imagines* was translated into French by de Vi-

genere: at least one edition (Paris, 1578) dates from before *A Midsummer Night's Dream* (Paris, 1614; L'Angelier rpt., New York: Garland, 1976). *Imagines* was extensively commented upon and quoted by Gyraldus and Cartari, whose *Le imagini dei degli antichi* often reads like a transcript of Philostratus. *Imagines* was highly esteemed by Shakespeare's fellow dramatists. Jonson directly quoted Philostratus six times in his abundant notes to his masques (i.e. in a note to "Cupids" in *The Masque of Beauty*, 1608: "especially *Phil.* in Icon. Amor. whom I haue particularly followed in this description." *Works*, Hereford and Simpson, ed. [Oxford: Oxford University Press, 1941], 7:188). See Allan H. Gilbert, *The Symbolic Persons in the Masques of Ben Jonson* (Durham, N.C.: Duke University Press, 1948), pp. 262–63. Samuel Daniel referred to *Imagines* and followed very precisely its image of Sleep in *The Vision of the Twelve Goddesses* (1604): "And therefore was Sleep/as he is described by Philostratus in *Amphiarai imagine*/apparelled." *A Book of Masques* (Cambridge: Cambridge University Press, 1967), p. 28.

53.   For over a hundred years commentaries suggested the source of the name Philostrate is borrowed from Chaucer's *The Knight's Tale*. But Chaucer's lover, who goes to Athens under the name of Philostrate, and Shakespeare's master of the revels have nothing in common. The author of *Imagines* as a possible source for the name of Philostrate is a guess one is tempted to make. Philostratus' "Comus" is generally thought to be the main source for the image of Comus opening Jonson's *Pleasure Reconcild to Vertue* (1618) and for Milton's *Comus* (1634). *A Midsummer Night's Dream* and the two plays have often been compared: Jonson's *Pleasure* with *Comus* (Paul Reyher, *Les Masques anglaises* [Paris, 1909; New York: B. Blom, 1964], pp. 212–13; Welsford, *The Court Masque*, pp. 314–20; the editors of Jonson, *Works*, 2:304–9); *A Midsummer Night's Dream* with *Comus* (Welsford, *The Court Masque*, pp. 330–35; Glynne Wickham, *Shakespeare's Dramatic Heritage* [London: Routledge & Kegan Paul, 1969], pp. 181–84). But the real link between these three plays is the passage on Comus in *Imagines* (1.2). See also Stephen Orgel, *The Jonsonian Masque* (Cambridge, Mass.: Harvard University Press, 1965), pp. 151–69. Orgel compares the passage on Comus from Philostratus with Cartari's *Le imagini* and describes the iconographic tradition stemming from *Imagines*.

54.   Fragment B 15. Quoted from Albert Cook, "Heraclitus and the Conditions of Utterance," *Arion*, n.s. 2/4 (1976): 473.

55.   Wind, "Orpheus," pp. 104, 158.

The Tempest, or Repetition

I. Plantation on a Mythical Island

The explorers and founders of the first colonies not only gave old world names—New England, New Amsterdam, New Orleans, Jamestown, and Virginia—to new lands and newly founded settlements, but they also identified their ocean voyages into uncharted territory and their discovery of new islands and lands with the journeys of Odysseus and Aeneas. Real history and real events were viewed and recreated in mythical terms and images such as the Argonauts' quest for the golden fleece or the return to paradise lost. In the first paintings and etchings representing the freshly discovered new world, such as Mostaert's *West Indian Scene,* the hills and woods of Umbria appear in pastoral landscapes, rabbits scurry away amid cows and sheep grazing on green slopes, and the naked inhabitants have the harmonious and athletic bodies of Greek and Roman warriors. In the travel diaries and descriptions of new lands, from Columbus and Peter Martyr to the reports from Virginia and the pilgrims' letters from New England, we find paraphrases from Virgil, Horace, and Ovid intermingled with the languages of sailors and colonizers.[1]

In all of sixteenth- and seventeenth-century travel literature, from ship's log to fantastic romances, we discover the same elementary opposition between the new idiom of experience and the language of the Bible or images from the *Aeneid.* In this mythic paradigm expeditions to the New World found their *arché* and providential theology. The very concept of a "new world" contains a basic contradiction between myth and history, repetition and novelty. The "new world," different from the "old," just recently discovered, is at the same time a prelapsarian garden, free from curse and cleansed of crime. The New World represents renewal. Awareness of this new beginning was deeply rooted in the ethos of the Puritan pilgrims, who settled the shores of New England. The New World was to be a purification. And there is no purification without myth.

Greek and Roman myths were Mediterranean. They contained not only the images of gods, heroes, and monsters, their names and their deeds, but also Mediterranean geography. Mythology is beyond time, but rarely beyond space. In the mythic geography of the Renaissance the Atlantic was transformed into the new Mediterranean; the West Indies replaced Crete, Lemnos, and Sicily. America was peopled by the terrifying and enchanting monsters of Africa.

Prospero's "uninhabited island" has two geographical locations. It lies both on Aeneas' sea route between Carthage/Tunis and Cumae/Naples and on the map of the New World near the Bermudas. The African hag Sycorax, pregnant with Caliban, sails from "Argier"; the "Mediterranean fleet" of Alonso, king of Naples, sails as Aeneas from Carthage/Tunis.

> GONZALO: This Tunis, sir, was Carthage.
> ADRIAN: Carthage?
> GONZALO: I assure you, Carthage.
> ANTONIO: His word is more than the miraculous harp.
>   (2.1.80–83)

Prospero's place is simultaneously a Mediterranean island of metamorphosis and penitence and a new plantation on the coast of America. "It is not down on any map; true places never are," wrote Melville about an island in *Moby Dick*. But Melville was only partly right: the mythical islands, "true places," can be found on maps of the Mediterranean.

Ariel disperses Alonso's ships at Prospero's commands just as Aeolus scatters Aeneas' ships at Juno's. Ferdinand emerges from the sea as did naked Odysseus, and Miranda, like white-shouldered Nausicaa, is enraptured by his beauty and believes him to be a god.

> I might call him
> A thing divine; for nothing natural
> I ever saw so noble.
>
> (1.2.420–422)[2]

Ariel's music draws Ferdinand just as the music of the Sirens tempted Odysseus' companions. "Where should this music be? I' th' air or th' earth? . . . I have follow'd it, / Or it hath drawn me rather" (1.2.390, 396–7). The mythical are evoked again when Ferdinand opposes their deceiving voices to Miranda's innocent charm: "and many a time / Th' harmony of their tongues hath into bondage / Brought my too diligent ear" (3.1.40–42).

Shakespeare took the most dangerous of Prospero's spells from Medea in Ovid's *Metamorphoses* and bestowed the remainder of her frightful charms on Sycorax. "This blue-ey'd hag" also resembles Circe. Mythical permutations are limited, however, and in Neoplatonic and hermetic texts, Medea and Circe, together or separately, always personify magic.[3]

The imaginary scenery of Prospero's island seems astonishingly similar to the tiny islet on the Carthaginian coast in the *Aeneid* to which the refugees from Troy swam after the shipwreck:[4]

> The great cliffs come down
> Steep to deep water, and the background shimmers,
> Darkens and shines, the tremulous aspen moving
> And the dark fir pointing still. And there is a cave
> With water running fresh, a home of the Nymphs.[5]

The eighteenth-century stage directions are evidently under the spell of Virgil: "The island. Low overgrown cliffs; among them the entrance to a high cell hung with drapery. A path running through a lemon grove and along the rocky slope leads directly to the cave." Rowe's directions state, "The island." Prospero's island has two imaginary connotations, which we could call the "Mediterranean connection" and the "Bermudas connection." On the emblematic stage of the Globe with the "Heavens" adorned with the signs of the zodiac, the "poor isle" was mythical and real at the same time. But even the real "Islands in the Bermudas, as every man knoweth that hath heard or read of them, were never inhabited by any Christian or heathen peoples, but were ever esteemed and reputed a most prodigious and enchanted place which offer nothing beyond hurricanes, storms, and devilish weather, so that every sailor and navigator avoids it like Scylla and Charybdis . . ."[6] Prospero's island could well have seemed real to the Globe's audience because of the fusing of the mythical tradition with news from travelers to the New World.

On one of the earliest maps of America, drawn by Alberto Cantino in 1502, a line on the blue sea divides Spanish possessions from the Portuguese. Three red parrots sit where Brazil is today, and Newfoundland is a green island with carefully designed tall trees which look like pines.[7] In such a tall pine tree Ariel was imprisoned by Sycorax.

Prospero subjected Ferdinand to a test of hunger and thirst. He commanded him to drink "sea-water" and to eat the "fresh-brook mussels" and "wither'd roots." A very refined diet. And, as additional fare, he prescribed "husks / wherein the acorn cradled" (1.2.466–67). In the golden age, as Ovid wrote in *Metamorphoses,* "acorns dropt on ground, from Jove's brode tree in fielde." From Ovid and Virgil to Petrarch and Spenser, the acorns fallen from the oaks consecrated to Jove were eaten in all Arcadias. But husks of acorn are inedible even in Arcadia. Prospero imposes upon Ferdinand an inedible Arcadian diet and the meager means of sustenance of lost travelers wandering the new continent. Two separate diets, two different culinary "systems," belong to the pastoral Arcadia and the savage one.[8]

In the "green world" of Shakespeare's comedies shepherds from pastoral Arcadia meet Elizabethan courtiers; the "forest" is at the same time near Athens and near Stratford. Perhaps this is why all "Arcadias" are so bitter, and the "Illyria" an illusion. The real world is ever-present, and in the last act there is no escape. Yet nowhere else are the mythical images so fused with the new Renaissance experience as in *The Tempest.* Poetry is ambiguous by its very nature; setting, costumes—even the bodies and faces of the actors—are, on stage, univocal by their very nature. And that is why *The Tempest* is the most difficult of all Shakespeare's plays to perform. Myths and the experience of the colonizers do not speak the same language. *The Tempest* is torn within and does not come together even at the end, neither in its realistic setting nor in the imagination. The theater must mark this split. But how? The bare stage of the Globe was the ideal setting for *The Tempest*.

Caliban probably owes his name as much to Montaigne's essay "On Cannibals" as he does to the "Carib" of the new land. Philosophers will soon propose "natural" man as an exemplary model but not before he has been enslaved by colonists. In *The Tempest*'s "Names of the Actors," Caliban figures as "a savage and deformed slave." Not the "noble savage" of the philosophers, he is a "monster" and slave. In mythical heritage, Caliban is a "monster." In the nomenclature of New World colonists, he is, of course, a "slave."

> Then was this island
> (Save for the son that she did litter here,
> A freckled whelp, hag-born) not honour'd with
> A human shape.
> (1.2.281–84)

Caliban has "a human shape," but he is "a freckled whelp hag-born." In the last scene Prospero calls him "disproportion'd in his manner / As in his shape" (5.1.290–91). The monster ("deformed," "disproportion'd") is a hybrid. In classical tradition, monsters were the fruit of forbidden and illicit relations between man and gods or between man and animals; in the Middle Ages, they were the offspring of liaisons between witches and the devil. Caliban, "this thing of darkness" (5.1.275) is the offspring of such "unnatural" relations: "got by the devil himself / Upon thy wicked dam" (1.2.321–22).[9] The medieval devil, who sired Caliban, has, in turn, been transformed into the god Setebos of Patagonia, mentioned by Pigafetta, who accompanied Magellan on his voyages.

In the mythical code of the hybrid bastard, only the names change. The Shakespearean monster spawned of the powers of evil and imprisoned in a cave for his groundless lust also has his Mediterranean genealogy: *hic crudelis amor tauri sup-*

*postaque furto/Pasiphae mistumque genus prolesque biformis/Min-
otaurus inest"* (*Aeneid*, 6, 24–26).

> the scene portrays
> Pasiphae in cruel love, the bull
> She took to her by cunning, and their offspring,
> The mongrel Minotaur, half man, half monster,
> The proof of lust unspeakable.

Caliban's hybrid nature is at the core of the mythical code
in *The Tempest*. "In every myth system," writes Edmund Leach,
"we will find a persistent series of binary discriminations as
between human/superhuman, mortal/immortal, male/fe-
male, legitimate/illegitimate, good/bad . . . followed by a mediation of paired categories thus distinguished. Mediation (in
this sense) is always achieved by introducing a third category
which is abnormal or anomalous in terms of ordinary rational
categories. Thus myths are full of fabulous monsters."[10]

Prospero is the last of Shakespeare's rulers in the double
role of exile and the new usurper. The Magus of the Renaissance hermetic tradition conforms exactly to this anomalous category of mediators, which does not fit the
opposition: lord's anointed / usurper. Caliban is both natural
man and slave. The mediating term here seems to be "fairy-
tale monster." Ariel, too, is a slave—"my slave" (1.2.271) Prospero calls him—but he is also the main actor in a psychodrama
on the "uninhabited" isle. The mediating term here, of course,
is "airy spirit."

Ariel is "light" and floats in the air. Caliban is heavy and
crawls as a turtle: "Come, thou tortoise!" (1.2.318). Or even
more emphatically: "Thou earth, thou!" (314). In these elemental mythic oppositions Caliban is of earth and water,
Ariel of air and fire. Caliban is formed of the "dust of the
ground"; Ariel, spirit of the air, is the "breath of life." Together they are the divided first man in Genesis. Only Shakespeare and Milton had this power of creation, both mythic
and realistic.

The Tempest has frequently invited allegorical interpretation. Myths operate on binary oppositions. In *The Tempest*
binary oppositions are significant, but ambiguous enough to

be translated into various mythological systems. In a certain sense, Prospero's "poor isle" is the island of all myths. The "anomalous" dual character of the three principal characters is necessary for the mythic mediation so that, in the course of one afternoon, the history can be repeated and the people cleansed of crime.

But the action of *The Tempest* is not confined to a mythic island. The education of this "natural man" takes place on one of the islands of the New World. Man "in the state of nature" is a savage, but "a noble savage" is now a cannibal. Nurture and Art are opposed to primeval nature corrupted from its very inception. "I must obey: his Art is of such pow'r" (1.2.374), says Caliban of Prospero; and Prospero describes Caliban as one "on whose nature / Nurture can never stick" (4.1.188–89). Art can tame nature, but nature does not submit to education, whether in Milan or in the Bermudas. The oppositions of Nature and Culture, savagery and community, are always more realistic and their confrontation more dramatic in Shakespeare than in Renaissance moral philosophy. The comic script of *The Tempest* draws from Plautus (as Bernard Knox has suggested) and from the *commedia dell'arte* the opposition of two servant/slaves—one clever, quick, and resourceful, the instigator of the action, like Ariel; and another, like Caliban, lazy and rebellious, "on whose nature / Nurture can never stick" (4.1.188–89), and like him flogged at the play's end.

The Tempest has often been interpreted as the education of the savage. "Thou . . . wouldst . . . teach me how / To name the bigger light, and how the less, / That burn by day, and night" (1.2.336). In this chapter of cultural anthropology the text distinctly reads, not how to renew, but "how to name."

Prometheus taught his "insect-men" to distinguish day from night and to measure time by phases of the moon. Caliban was taught "the language." But what "language"?

MIRANDA: I pitied thee,
Took pains to make thee speak, taught thee each hour
One thing or other. When thou didst not, savage,
Know thine own meaning, but wouldst gabble like
A thing most brutish, I endow'd thy purposes

With words that make them known. . .
CALIBAN: You taught me language. . .

(1.2.354–60, 368)

"You taught me language. . ." Was Caliban "a creature of nature" like the animals, not blessed with the gift of speech, or did he speak his own tongue before he learned a language from the planters?[11] Your language . . .

"The red plague rid you/For learning me *your* language" (1.2.366–67). The drunken sailors were taken aback: "Where the devil should he learn *our* language?" (2.2.67–68, my italics). The "natural man" learned the curses from his masters. Stephano calls him a "monster." But this creature, smelling like fish, under whose cloak hides a pretender to the title of viceroy,[12] now has four legs as in the *lazzi* of *commedia dell'arte*. The mythical monster has been transformed into an antic one: "Legg'd like a man! and his fins like arms! Man o' my troth! . . . this is not fish, but an islander . . ." (2.2.34–37).

This comical creature, whose short and soaked "gabardine" exposes his bare legs, was taken for a native. Trinculo, a man of the world, sees Caliban as a sideshow attraction that could earn him a fortune anywhere, but most certainly in England: "when they will not give a doit to relieve a lame beggar, they will lay out ten to see a dead Indian" (2.2.31–34).[13]

According to Malone's account, Caliban's costume, "which doubtless was prescribed by the poet himself and has been continued . . . since his time, is a large bear skin, or the skin of some other animal; and he is usually represented with long shaggy hair." This was a strange costume for an "Indian." In adaptations of *The Tempest* from the Restoration period to almost the end of the nineteenth century Caliban was invariably represented on stage as a "primitive man," "half a fish and half a monster" (3.2.28). In Daniel Chodowiecki's late eighteenth-century illustrations of *The Tempest*, Caliban is shown as an aquatic creature with the head of a giant toad. Even as late as 1871 in London's Queens Theatre, Caliban was played with enormous cardboard teeth and jaw.[14] The only exception to this scenographic and iconographic tradition known to me is the frontispiece appearing in both the 1773 and 1774 English editions of *The Tempest* by Bell. A kneeling Caliban drinks greedily from a flask handed to him by Stephano. The caption: "Come on then. Down, and swear!" Caliban is naked except for a feathered loincloth. He has Negroid features. But even this realistic "savage" with black skin has claws on his feet and hands.

The first American "savages" brought to Bristol in 1501 were "clothid in beastys skinnys . . . ete Rave Flesh" and behaved like "bruyt beastis." Alberto Cantino, who saw them a year earlier in Lisbon, wrote that they had "the most bestial manners and habits, like wild men." *The True Declaration* (1610), which was, indisputably, a source for *The Tempest*, describes the natives of Virginia as "human beasts," and Captain John Smith, almost in the same year, calls them "perfidious, inhuman, all savage." Prospero calls Caliban a "dull thing" even before we see him on the stage. Even sweet Miranda spares him no invective: an "abhorred slave," of a "vile race," "a thing most brutish." This is already a new colonial English idiom. Prospero and Miranda are speaking the language of Captain Smith when they call Caliban from his cave which they have designated as his lair.

PROSPERO: We'll visit Caliban, my slave, who never
   Yields us kind answer.
MIRANDA: 'Tis a villain, sir,
   I do not love to look on.
PROSPERO: But as 'tis,
   We cannot miss him: he does make our fire,
   Fetch in our wood, and serves in offices
   That profit us.

                        (1.2.310–15)

The "uninhabited island" is a place of magic, penance, and purification. But Shakespeare transforms the mythic island, peopled with nymphs, monsters, and witches, into a plantation of the New World.

    Had I plantation of this isle, my lord—
    . . .
    I would with such perfection govern, sir,
    T' excel the Golden Age.
            (2.1.140, 163–64)

The word "plantation" was used only once by Shakespeare and that was in *The Tempest*. This word was new, introduced into English a little more than fifty years before *The
Tempest*.[15] In Gonzalo's musings on a utopian community only
twenty-four lines divide "plantation" from "the golden age."
In the same scene, in this terse syntagm, two "languages"
meet and collide with each other: of utopia and of
experience.[16]

> GONZALO: Had I plantation of this isle, my lord . . .
> All things in common Nature should produce
> Without sweat or endeavour . . .
>   . . . but Nature should bring forth,
> Of it own kind, all foison, all abundance,
> To feed my innocent people.
> SEBASTIAN: No marrying 'mong his subjects?
> ANTONIO: None, man; All idle; whores and knaves.
>   (2.1.155–6, 158–62)

In 1606, barely five years before *The Tempest*, Michael
Drayton described the new Arcadia rediscovered in a plantation of Virginia as an unending holiday of bounty in his
ode "Earth's onely Paradise."[17]

> Where Nature hath in store
> Fowle, Venison and Fish,
> And the Fruitfull'st Soyle,
> Without your Toyle.
> Three Harvest more
> All greater than you wish.

Almost the same images were invoked by Ceres in the masque
conjured up by Prospero on the uninhabited island for Ferdinand and Miranda.

> Earth's increase, foison plenty,
> Barns and garners never empty,
> Vines with clust'ring bunches growing,
> Plants with goodly burden bowing . . .
>   (4.1.110–13)

Drayton's ode was dedicated to "the Virginian voyage."
In this "Earth's Onely Paradise," history once again returned
to its mythical beginning: "the golden age / Still natures lawes
doth give . . ." The New World is the biblical garden of abun-

dance from which the first parents were exiled, the golden age, which had returned.[18] Utopia is the mythical past projected into the future. "Utopia" means "a place, which does not exist." But in 1516 Thomas More imagined his Utopia on one of the islands close to the West Indies archipelago newly discovered by Vespucci. The inhabitants of the first Renaissance utopia knew nothing of property and did not know what violence was. They were equal and happy.[19]

"Had I plantation of this isle, my lord . . ."

> Letters should not be known; riches, poverty,
> And use of service, none . . .
> No occupation; all men idle, all;
> And women too, but innocent and pure;
> No sovereignty. . .
>   (2.1.146–47, 149–52)

The influence of Florio's new translation of Montaigne has often been pointed out in this vision of the ideal plantation. But the noble-minded counselor was equally well-read in Virgil, Ovid, and Renaissance adventure stories which were read greedily in the second half of the sixteenth century when English voyages to the New World began. Gonzalo in his discourse utilizes the well-known classical rhetorical device of consecutive negations. The garden of Eden, the golden age, and the utopian colony are imagined as a simple inversion of unhappy civilization corrupted by excess, privileges, and luxury.

Before his expedition to Tunis-Carthage, Gonzalo might have read *De orbe novo decades,* translated in 1555, in which Peter Martyr describes the innocent life of the West Indies islanders: "A few things content them, having no delight in such superfluities for which in other places menne take infinite paynes, and commit manie unlawfull actes. . . . But among these simple soules, a fewe clothes serve the naked: weightes and measures are not needful to such as cannot skill of craft and deceite, and have not the use of pestiferous money, . . . they seeme to live in that golden worlde of the whiche olde writers speake so much, wherein menne lived simply and innocently without enforcements of lawes, without quarreling, judges, and libelles, content only to satisfie nature . . ."[20]

"Had I plantation of this isle, my lord . . ." The power of the classical text is astounding. Martyr, who translated the letters and diaries of Columbus and Vespucci into Latin for the Pope and his humanistic circles, trusted more in Virgil than in the navigators who traversed thousands of sea miles in fragile ships to get to the already discovered new paradisaic gardens of delight. In his reports about the inhabitants of Hispañola, today's Haiti, Martyr employed the same stylistic device of successive negation that Ovid used in his *Metamorphoses* when describing the golden age. Shakespeare probably read this famous passage in Latin when he was still in school, but he may also have known it in Golding's translation from the year 1567.

> There was no fear of punishment, there was no threatening
> lawe,
> In brazen tables nayled up, to keepe folke in awe.
> There was no man would crouch or creepe to Judge with cap
> in hand,
> They lived safe without a Judge, in everie Realme and
> lande. . .
> No horne nor trumpet was in use, no sword nor helmet
> worne,
> The worlde was such, that soldiers helpe might easily be
> forborne.
> The fertile earth as yet was free . . .
> (*The First Booke*, 105–8, 113–15)

But there is also an anti-utopian trend in Renaissance literature and in the accounts of voyagers to the New World, which has its roots in another tradition. The first to visit the inhospitable Arcadia of barbaric herdsmen of goats and sheep was the tireless traveler Odysseus: "The Cyclopes have no assemblies for the making of laws, nor any settled customs, but live in hollow caverns in the mountain heights, where each man is lawgiver to his children and his wives, and nobody cares a jot for his neighbors" (*Odyssey* 9.105 ff.).

Led by an unbridled curiosity (not unlike that of today's anthropologists, who should elect him their patron), Odysseus decided to see for himself how this community, so unlike all others he had visited, rules itself. "I want you to stay here, while I go in my own ship with my own crew to find out what kind of men are over there and whether they are brutal and lawless savages or hospitable and god-fearing people" (9.173 ff.).

He took a goatskin of the best wine, let himself down into the cave, and, like Trinculo, determined to get the monster drunk. The drunk Cyclops abducted Odysseus' two companions, tore them to pieces, and made himself a supper of them. Odysseus saved himself and his companions by a linguistic operation. When the Cyclops asked what his name was, he answered, "Nobody." In the ruckus caused by the blinded potentate, his neighbors came to ask why he did not let them sleep. Polyphemus cried from the cave that nobody blinded him. Perhaps only semanticists can fully appreciate this use for the first time in the history of literature and logic of the empty class (or a signifier without a designate) as one's own name.

Odysseus left the island of the Cyclops free of all illusions and knew for certain that a society contemptuous of law and ignorant of agriculture and industry by no means resembles the golden age but rather consists of cannibals devouring unwary visitors. These two Arcadias, the idyllic and the barbaric, are both notions of "nature" in a pure state.[21]

"Had I plantation of this isle, my Lord . . ." Hardly has Gonzalo, amidst the jibes of the royal retinue, finished his musings about innocent societies living in the womb of a benevolent nature ("How lush and lusty the grass looks! how green!" [2.1.51]), than a scene from an Elizabethan tragedy commences on the fragrant and lush grass of a Virgilian Arcadia. Fratricide and regicide are prevented only through Ariel's spells. The "time of the murderers" (*le temps des assassins*) has come to the mythical isle. History is stronger than myth in Shakespeare.

"No sovereignty," "all things in common"—Gonzalo, enchanted by his own loquaciousness, repeats his classics lesson: "These natives enjoy a golden age, for they know neither *meum* nor *teum*," wrote Peter Martyr of the "good savages" in Cuba. Into his uninhabited colony Prospero introduced property: the division between "mine" and "thine": "*My* slave," "*our* fire," "offices that profit *us*" (my italics).

"In the 'majestic vision' of the Golden Age which Prospero unfolded before the young couple, Ariel and the spirits played the roles of three goddesses. When the masque is suddenly interrupted, they dissolve into thin air. But they return again in new shapes. In the last metamorphosis of this new Ovid Prospero and Ariel unleash these very spirits transformed into hunting dogs upon two rebel sailors and an Indian slave."[22] This is one of the most frightening scenes in *The Tempest*, yet its theatrical cruelty was never shown onstage:

> PROSPERO: Fury, Fury! There, Tyrant, there! Hark, hark!
> (*Caliban, Stephano, and Trinculo are driven out*)
>   Go, charge my goblins that they grind their joints
>   With dry convulsions, shorten up their sinews
>   With aged cramps, and more pinch-spotted make them
>   Then pard or cat o'mountain.
> ARIEL: Hark, they roar!
> PROSPERO: Let them be hunted soundly.
>
> (4.1.257–62)

Caliban twice calls Prospero a tyrant: "A plague upon the tyrant that I serve!" (2.2.162) and in act 3: "I am subject to a tyrant" (3.2.40). One of the hunting dogs that Prospero sets on the slave is called "Tyrant." The lord of the plantation, called by his slave a "tyrant," is now in this violent parallel transformed into a hound. On this plantation near the Bermudas the rebels assume animal form under the spell of Ariel's horrifying music. He beats his drums for them: "At which, like unback'd colts, they prick'd their ears, / Advanc'd their eyelids, lifted up their noses / As they smelt music" (4.1.176–78). Now left in the dungwater, they will have to await mercy.

In this brutal dramaturgy arguments are actions and oppositions. The evocation of a utopian community ends in an attempt to murder the sleeping rulers; the vision of a harvest without human toil changes into a manhunt. By the end of act 4, Prospero's plantation has become Circe's island where Odysseus' companions were transformed into hogs. But this new island of the old Circe appears at the end of the Renaissance, when the "brave new world" turns out to be a repetition of all the crimes and madness of the old. "The unpredictable, the abnormal, the inhuman, the cruel, the savage and the strange in terms of European experience," writes H. M. Jones, "were from the beginning part of the image of a land that was ours before we were the land's. The New World was filled with monsters animal and monsters human . . ." This is nearly a paradigm of *The Tempest.*[23]

On the engraving *Columbus Landing in the Indies* (1493), a king, probably the Spanish Ferdinand, crowned and holding a scepter, sits in the foreground on a splendid throne placed at the edge of the ocean and watches a small galley approach the shores of the new land graced by one tall palm tree and naked, dancing savages. The ocean, which divides the Old World from the New World, is depicted as a narrow strait. The dramatic innovation of *The Tempest* is to set the old feudal drama on one of the islands of the New World. Not only do the great myths of paradise lost and the golden age come to the "uninhabited island," but Shakespeare's tragic themes of the Lord's anointed and the usurper are reenacted there.

From this new and broad perspective, the history of the last of Shakespeare's rulers is once again the history of the world. Prospero, like Aeneas, founds a plantation in a new land and, like Odysseus, returns to his Ithaca. The mythical story repeats itself as universal history. But in these two histories the homecoming is bitter. The utopia turns out to be as impossible in the Old World as on the mythical island of the New. In court masques from the Elizabethan and Stuart period, goddesses come down from Olympus and bless the bride and groom. Courtiers, dressed as Arcadian shepherds, celebrate the arrival of the golden age. But in *The Tempest* a wedding masque is as ominously interrupted as the nuptials of Dido and Aeneas in the *Aeneid.* The Renaissance read the fourth book of the *Aeneid* as the tragedy of the "widow Dido." Shakespeare is the first to read it as the tragedy of the "widower Aeneas."

Macbeth and *Hamlet* are more cruel than *The Tempest. King Lear* is a tragedy without hope: the world has fallen to pieces and will never grow back together again. Yet *The Tempest* has always seemed to me the saddest of Shakespeare's plays. There is in it, even more than in *Doctor Faustus,* the bitter taste of lost hope. There is a metaphysical uneasiness in both of these dramas that eludes interpretation and is difficult to name. Yet one cannot free oneself from Prospero's despair any more than one can elude the memory of clinical death. No one can avoid reading *The Tempest* as the story of his own defeat.

Mythical and real history were played out in the course of one short afternoon on these "unhappy (yet happy) islands," as the Bermudas were called in *The True Declaration.* Ariel called the island on which he was imprisoned "the most forlorn" (2.3.80); Prospero calls it "bare" in the epilogue.

> Now my charms are all o'erthrown,
> And what strength I have's mine own,
> Which is most faint . . .
>   (Epilogue, 1–3)

Virgil called Aeneas *pius.* If piety is obedience to destiny, to the end and beyond the loss of illusions, then the "widower" Prospero was also pious. Like Aeneas he had survived the "wreckage of the world" and he had seen *lacrimae rerum.*

> And my ending is despair,
> Unless I be reliev'd by prayer,
> Which pierces so, that it assaults
> Mercy itself, and frees all faults.
>   (Epilogue, 15–18)

As in Virgil and Dante, both human souls and human history go through purgatory.

II. The Three Hours, or Purgatory

"At least two glasses. The time 'twixt six and now / Must by us both be spent most preciously" (1.2.240–41). The sixth hour, at which the plot draws to a close, is evoked by Ariel near the end of the play: "On the sixth hour; at which time, my lord, / You said our work should cease" (5.1.4–5). This duration must have had particular significance to Shakespeare since he refers to it twice more in the last scene; through Alonso ("Your eld'st acquaintance cannot be three hours" [5.1.186]) and through the Boatswain ("Our ship / Which, but three glasses since, we gave out split / Is tight" [5.1.222–24]). The Boatswain has remained on the ship with the sailors and did not participate in the events on the enchanted island; he now arrives from the outside, offering his measure of time as an objective witness. It is the same three hours.

These three hours between the past and the future are a time of transformation. In Renaissance symbolism three hours signify a "vestige of the Trinity," the unity of the past, present, and future.[24] ". . . Whereof, what's past is Prologue" (2.1.248). The future is the epilogue. The past evoked in *The Tempest* is divided into two periods, each twelve years long. The hag Sycorax comes to the island pregnant, and Caliban is born on the island. Twelve years later, and twelve years before the tempest of the prologue, Prospero lands on the island with Miranda. For twelve years Caliban was the hereditary ruler of the island, and for the following twelve years, he was Prospero's slave. "For I am all the subjects that you have, / Which first was mine own king" (1.2.341). For twelve years Ariel suffered unbearable tortures while imprisoned by Sycorax and then served Prospero another twelve years to earn his promised freedom. Miranda was three years old when she came to the island with her father, and in order to complete the symmetry, Prospero should have been duke of Milan for twelve years, just as for the next twelve years he was an exile and usurper on the island.

In Neoplatonic doctrine, the number twelve is a symbol of cosmic order and salvation. The zodiac has twelve signs, and twelve is also indicated by the wheel drawn by the magus' compass. But this hermetic symbolism is not necessary here: twelve is the measure of hours and months during which time is repeated. The past is the prologue of *The Tempest* and the history of brothers exiling brothers and of rulers deprived of thrones by usurpers. The present time in *The Tempest*, three hours of action on stage, are accelerated in the violently dramatic repetition of royal history.

Sebastian and Antonio draw their swords to kill the sleeping king of Naples and the new duke of Milan. ". . . As thou got'st Milan, / I'll come by Naples. Draw thy sword. One stroke / Shall free three from the tribute which thou payest" (2.1.285–

88). Regicide is enacted twice onstage in *The Tempest*, the first time with all the horror of a tragedy, and the second time as a scoffing farce, when Caliban and two drunks sneak up to kill the sleeping Prospero: ". . . Do the murther first: if he awake, / From toe to crown he'll fill our skins with pinches/ Make us strange stuff" (4.1.232–33). Yet there is also a third, "innocent" usurper in *The Tempest*. The noble Ferdinand proclaims himself king of Naples: "thou dost here usurp/ The name thou ow'st not" (1.2.456–57). In a moment he will attack Prospero with his sword.

In addition to these three spectacular attempts, played onstage before the audience, there is also the symbolic dethroning by the forces of nature in the prologue to the play. The elements of fire and water are not obedient to royal commands, and not even the most powerful of the anointed sovereigns can command an ordinary storm to cease. "What cares these roarers for the name of King?" (1.1.16–17). Most significant is the symmetry of two cries: Antonio's: "Let's all sink wi' th' King," and Sebastian's replay like a sinister forecast of the future: "Let's take leave of him" (1.1.62, 63).

The beginning is the end and the end is the beginning. After the second cycle of twelve years and after three hours of Prospero's theatrical magic, Caliban and Ariel return to point zero, where the plot began, so that all the events can be reenacted. The past returned to Prospero's island on a ship which came from Naples and now, on the very same ship, everyone will return to Naples: the exile along with those who exiled him. The uninhabited island will once more become Caliban's domain, and Ariel will be free to reunite with the elements.

In *The Tempest* time reverts to its beginning through the recurrence and repetition of past events: three times measured on the hourglass. The hourglass is an image of returning time. When the sand runs out, the hourglass is turned upside down and the same sand runs its course again. Each hour measured by the sand is a different hour and the same hour.

The beginning is the end and the end is a new beginning. "The epic," writes Thomas M. Greene, "is the great poem of beginnings and endings. The *Aeneid* is typical, beginning with an ending and ending with a beginning."[25] Aeneas' route leads from the city which was destroyed to the city which was to be built. In the great plan of the *Aeneid* the first six books are the repetition of the *Odyssey,* and the next six of the *Iliad.* There is a repetition not only of the epic pattern but of the myth as well. History, in order to renew itself, must repeat itself as myth.

Aeneas must repeat Odysseus' journey and stand at the walls of Latium, just as the Greeks stood at the walls of Troy. In this renewal of history through repetition the myth repeats itself, but its signs are inverted. Aeneas journeys not to the East but to the West; he does not, like Odysseus, return to the home which he had left, but leaves the home which he has lost and journeys to build a new home in a new land. In the *Aeneid,* the *Iliad* follows the *Odyssey.* The vanquished turns into victor: Aeneas, the new Achilles, kills Turnus, the new Hector.[26]

The past in the *Aeneid* returns not only symbolically in Homeric parallelisms and similes and not only in Aeneas' tales of the destruction of Troy (in the second book; the first book begins with the description of the storm). The past returns also like a reflection arrested in a mirror. The frescoes in the temple of Juno, which Dido built in Carthage, depicted all the battles fought under the walls of Troy, in order, one after the other. Aeneas recognized himself in these paintings "hotly engaged among the Greek chieftains" (1.488) and "sighed a deep and terrible sigh." He met his past.

In this striking artistic device, the flashback is discovered—a dramatic and spectacular return of the past. Aeneas sees Achilles dragging Hector's body around the walls of the city, and Priam supplicating the murderers. In Shakespeare's tragedies, the essence of history is regicide and an endless parade of rightful rulers and usurpers. The essence of Roman history in the *Aeneid* is destroyed cities and the cities to be built anew. In this the *Aeneid* is closer to us than the royal tragedies.

Aeneas visits the land of the dead just as Odysseus had. Homer's Hades is as unchanging as his world. The shadows of the dead are frozen in their pasts, their clothes are those which they wore in the days of their glory, and they repeat the same futile gestures. The dead, frozen in their life stories, learn nothing after their deaths and find out nothing new. They are inert memory, which nothing will change. In this Hades to which Odysseus descends, there is no punishment or reward, except that meted out to heroes who offended the gods of Olympus. The dead stroll in this sad prison-icebox, where nothing happens anymore. They are shadows of the living. Homer's Hades is a shadow of the world.

In Virgil's Hades there are heavenly gardens of happiness, a hell of tortures, and a pre-Christian purgatory of penance, oblivion, and renewal. The souls there, as in a long and painful bath, cleanse themselves of all traces of temporal life until, unburdened of the specters of the past, they attain forgetfulness and are ready for a new journey.

Standing on a hill as if on the upper level of the stage, Anchises shows his son Aeneas "the greatest gathering of souls" in a long queue for their return to earth and their new lives. The reincarnation of souls follows Plato's tale of Er, son of Armenius, in the last book of *The Republic*. But the purgatory where Anchises acts as Aeneas' guide, just as thirteen centuries later Virgil will be Dante's, is not only Platonic but Roman. The reincarnation of souls is also a reincarnation of history, in which Trojan fate is transformed into the history of Rome: from Sylvius, the late son of Aeneas, to Numa, the first king; and from Julius Caesar to Caesar Augustus. History in this Roman underground returns and renews itself just as it does on the surface of the earth and sea in Aeneas' journey from Troy to Latium. In this Hades, the past perfect tense changes into the future perfect.

Shakespeare could have had this gallery of kings and caesars from *Aeneid* 6 in mind when, as in the Virgilian cave of Sibyl, the three "weird sisters" conjure before Macbeth a procession of future kings of Scotland and England.

During the three hours on the "uninhabited" island, as in the Virgilian Hades, the past painfully turns into the future. Along the way, the "three men of sin" encounter Harpies, hear horrifying prophecies, and are subject to the tortures of hunger, thirst, and fear. Muddled and lost, they await mercy: "Who was so firm, so constant, that this coil / Would not infect his reason?" (1.2.207–8).

Ferdinand, betrothed to Miranda, thanks Prospero for a "second life." This "second life" has the ring of a "Christian Virgil." Even the insensitive Ariel, the executor of the punishment, took pity upon men:

> ARIEL: Your charm so strongly works 'em
>   That if you now beheld them, your affections
>   Would become tender.
> PROSPERO: Dost thou think so, spirit?
> ARIEL: Mine would, sir, were I human.

(5.1.17–20)

Within the mythic order, which repeats the Virgilian code, *The Tempest* ends with an act of forgiveness and renewal: *renovatio.*

>   in one voyage
> Did Claribel her husband find at Tunis
> And Ferdinand, her brother, found a wife
> Where he himself was lost, Prospero his dukedom
> In a poor isle, and all of us ourselves
> When no man was his own.

(5.1.208–13)

The journey through purgatory is over. Prospero invites the sinners, whose food was snatched away by the Harpies, to spend the night in his cell. The next day all of them will sail for Naples, the Virgilian Cumae. From the Middle Ages to the late Renaissance, the *Aeneid* was like Holy Writ, a canonical text and simultaneously its translation and interpretation, *mythos* and theology, a universal history and its Roman model.

> Arms and the man I sing, the first who came,
> Compelled by fate, an exile out of Troy,
> To Italy and the Lavinian coast

(*Aeneid* 1.1–5)

In the *Aeneid* the key word is *fatum.*

> Driven by fate and fortune, which no man
> Can cope with or escape.

(*Aeneid* 8.1–2)

Aeneas, the bearer of this historical *fatum*, is reminded unceasingly by his father, his divine mother, and all the executors of his destiny between Heaven and Earth: "*nate dea, quo fata trahunt retrahunt sequamur*" (8.334). This Roman *fatum* is *inexorable* (*Georgics* 2.491) and *ineluctable* (*Aeneid* 8. 334).

At the interrupted banquet, which repeats the scene with the Harpies from the *Aeneid*, Ariel calls himself and the Shapes accompanying him "Ministers of Fate." *Fatum* has yet another name in this scene, Destiny:

> You are three men of sin, whom destiny,
> That hath to instrument this lower world
> And what is in't . . .
>
> (3.3.53—55)

The *Iliad* ends before the final destruction of Troy, the *Aeneid* begins with the destruction of Troy and ends before the conquest of Latium. Before Aeneas can marry Lavinia and lay the foundation for the new city, a new Hector has to die at the walls of the old city. Everything must recur in order to begin again. The beginning is the end and the end a new beginning.

The Roman *fatum* led from cities changed into ashes to cities founded on ashes. "Destiny" in the royal tragedies was no less cruel. The usurper of the dukedom of Milan, torn away from his own brother, tries to persuade the other royal brother to repeat this relentless history of rulers who murder and are murdered.

> And that by destiny, to perform an act
> Whereof what's past is prologue . . .
>
> (2.1.247—48)

In Shakespeare, "fate," "destiny," and "providence" belong to a different semantic order.

> MIRANDA: How came we ashore?
> PROSPERO: By Providence divine . . .
>   Some food we had, and some fresh water
>
> (1.2.158—60)

Tragic "fate" and mythical "destiny" are replaced by providence in the comic layer of *The Tempest*. The "Providence

divine" of the comedy, with also "some food and some water,"
has always been marriage, which brings two feuding families
together.

FERDINAND: Sir, she is mortal;
But by immortal Providence she's mine.

                                                  (5.1.188–89)

Prospero renounced his magical art even before the in-
tervention of that truly "immortal" providence. He draws a
circle in the sand and utters incantations for the last time.
Neither white magic nor black is of any use anymore, and
even the art of the theater is no longer needed. The Magus
breaks his wand and buries it. The book of secret knowledge
rests at the bottom of the sea "deeper than did ever plummet
sound" (5.1.56), the exact depth at which, as Alonso feared,
Ferdinand's body rested, "deeper than e'er plummet sounded"
(3.2.101).

The caduceus and a hermetic book were instruments of
mediation through Art. Ferdinand replaces the instruments
of magic. Real mediation is achieved through marriage, which
is the oldest and longest-lasting repetition of the same story.
In this exchange of semantics and props, comedy replaces
tragedy in *The Tempest*.

MIRANDA: O wonder!
How many goodly creatures are there here!
How beauteous mankind is! O brave new world,
That has such people in't!
PROSPERO: 'Tis new to thee.

                                                  (5.1.181–84)

Three villains stood before Miranda: Antonio, the usurper of the dukedom of Milan; Alonso, his royal protector;
and his brother Sebastian, who on this island of the new world
attempts to commit the two oldest crimes: fratricide and regicide. " 'Tis new to thee." This "brave new world," to which
Huxley alludes in the title of his jeering anti-utopia, is nothing
new to Prospero.

The *Aeneid* is the story of renewal and the renewal of
history. Yet even before the Renaissance the renewal of history in the *Aeneid* was read as if it were mere repetition. But

the bitterest reading of the *Aeneid* seems to be contained in *The Tempest*. Three hours on the "uninhabited" island are purgatory, but this new purgatory of the late Renaissance differs from the Virgilian and the Dantean one.

The mythic purification in the *Aeneid* is only an illusion in *The Tempest*, just like the utopian plantation and the return of the Golden Age in this "brave new world."

Prospero's hermetic knowledge does not help him in the art of ruling. The library brings about his downfall. "I / Thus neglecting worldly ends, all dedicated / to closeness, and the bettering of my mind" (1.2.89–90). He read too much, but, unfortunately, he did not read *The Prince*. A stranger in his own country, he loses his dukedom. The most prized books of his Renaissance library go into exile with him. In Shakespeare's powerful dramatic logic, the hermetic books, which cause Prospero's downfall as duke of Milan, serve to give him power over Ariel and Caliban on the "uninhabited island." In the end, however, Prospero's library turns out to be as useless on the "uninhabited" island as it was in Milan. The education of Caliban, who is now one of Prospero's subjects, ends in another defeat: "A devil, a born devil, on whose nature / Nurture can never stick! on whom my pains, / Humanely taken, all, all lost, quite lost!" (4.1.188–90). In the twilight of the Renaissance neither "rough magic" nor "potent Art" nor even "heavenly music" softens the hearts of sinners or changes the course of history. Renaissance paradigms of the discovery of the New World represented not only Aeneas' voyage to the West, but journeys to the Promised Land and Jerusalem.[27] The first line in the Prophecies of *Isaiah* 29, like the first line of the *Aeneid*, speaks of a destroyed city. "Woe to Ariel, to Ariel, the city where David dwelt . . . Yet I will distress Ariel, and there shall be heaviness and sorrow: and it shall be unto me as Ariel." "Ariel"—"altar" or "Divine lion"—is a symbol of Jerusalem, the destroyed temple and the promised land.

Symbolic paradigms allow themselves to be exchanged, and the biblical Ariel of the destroyed city enriches the Virgilian parallel in *The Tempest*. But traditional philology is not only more modest than allegorical interpretation, it also seems more sure. In the first Folio we read: "Ariell, an ayrie spirit" or "Are melted into Ayre, into thin Ayre." "Ayre" and "Ayrie" are repeated eleven times in *The Tempest*. Ariel is air.

Myths always accompany the discoveries of the New World. The first American astronaut read from the first chapter of Genesis a message to the earth when his spaceship entered its orbit around the moon: "And the earth was without form, and void; and darkness was upon the face of the deep. And the spirit of God moved upon the face of the waters." For one instant the image of the Earth in the first day of creation appeared on the television screen. But over the waters and lands of this Earth, which by now was just another planet, rose not the spirit of God, but a spaceship. In cosmos, the linear concept of top and bottom no longer existed. But on the frontier of myths, tradition, and scientific discoveries, a newly discovered moon of Uranus was called Ariel.

In the *Aeneid* the past becomes the future through repetition. In *The Tempest,* too, time turns backward and the past is repeated. In this shortest of Shakespeare's plays (after *The Comedy of Errors*), key words and almost entire lines, situations, and theatrical signs repeat themselves.

The Tempest is also the most musical of Shakespeare's plays, in which parts are assigned to voices as to instruments in a musical score. *The Tempest* should be read not only in its diachronic and syntagmatic lines but as an orchestral score, with synchrony, recurrent themes, and counterpoint. Repetitions and inversion are full of meaning: in a certain sense, they form the philosophical message and theatrical core of *The Tempest.*

In the second scene of act 1, Miranda does not yet know about herself, her father, or the old world.

MIRANDA: What *foul play* had we, that we came from thence?
Or *bless'd* was't we did?
PROSPERO: Both, both, my girl:
By *foul play*, as thou say'st, were we heav'd thence,
But *blessedly* holp hither.
                              (1.2.60–63, my italics)

Repetitions in *The Tempest* entail a reversal of a relation and at the same time its completion. As in a folk tale, echo cues and fills in the hidden sense.[28] In act 5 Miranda plays chess with Ferdinand:

MIRANDA: Sweet lord, you play me *false*.
FERDINAND: No, my dearest love,
   I would not for the world.

                              (5.1.172–73, my italics)

Chess, the royal game, stands here for a ploy to win the kingdom.[29] Chess ends with a checkmate, the surrender of a king. This is the last regicide in *The Tempest*. The unexpected meaning emerging from the conversation at the chessboard reveals it as a repetition of the conversation between Miranda and her father in act 1. In *The Tempest* both tragedy and comedy (exchange between a legitimate ruler and a usurper; love of a daughter and a son of two divided families) constitute a transition from *"foul play"* to *"fair play"* or, if we want to continue reading Shakespeare's bitter wisdom, to Ferdinand's new *"foul play"* which will now be called *"fair play."*[30] Miranda has not yet become the wife of a ruler, has not yet left the "uninhabited island," and already she has agreed to *"foul play."* "Yes, for a score of kingdoms you should wrangle, / And I would call it *fair play*" (5.1.174–75), my italics). In this game, whose stakes are the kingdom, Ferdinand is blessed by his bride, two royal fathers and heaven itself: "Look down, you gods, / And on this couple drop a blessed crown!" (5.1.201–2).

The system of repetitions reveals the latent structure of the play, relates all characters, and reduces them to the common denominator of the universal experience of life and history.

All *torment, trouble, wonder* and *amazement*
Inhabits here
                              (5.1.104–5; my italics)

This is the image of purgatory through which the newcomers to the island and its inhabitants passed in the course of three hours. All "key-words" spoken by Gonzalo in this collective formula were previously distributed among the voices.[31] Ariel and Caliban were both subjected to *"torment"* (the word occurs eight times in the text). Prospero mentions

Ariel's torment three times: "Dost thou forget / From what a torment I did free thee?" (1.2.250–51); and twice more in the same scene (1.2.287, 289). When Caliban encountered Trinculo for the first time he mistook him for an evil spirit sent by Prospero: "here comes a spirit of his, and to torment me" (2.2.15). Fear, pains, and "torment" are transitive in *The Tempest*. Caliban thought that Trinculo was Ariel in disguise. Three more times he begs the spirit not to "torment" him.

Thoughts of Miranda's fate caused Prospero much pain and *"trouble"* during their sea journey from Milan: "What trouble / Was I then to you" (1.2.151–52). When the "masque" ends Prospero learns about Caliban's plot, and suddenly confesses to Ferdinand: "my old brain is troubled" (4.1.159).

Miranda was *"a wonder"* to Ferdinand when he saw her for the first time on the "uninhabited" island. To Caliban the drunken Trinculo appeared an equal "wonder." "A most ridiculous monster, to make a wonder of a poor drunkard!" (2.2.160). Alonso will also consider his first glimpse of the live Ferdinand playing chess with Miranda a "wonder" (5.1.169). And Miranda will exclaim: "O, wonder!" (5.1.182) when she sees the newcomers to the island in the last scene.

In *"amazement"* there is "wonder," "strangeness," and "fear." The sight of the sinking ship arouses amazement and fear in Miranda: "Be collected; / No more amazement" (1.2.13–14). This is Ariel's work: "I flam'd amazement" (1.2.198). The root of the English word amazement is "maze," confusion, bewilderment, and labyrinth. For Maynard Mack, the key image in *The Tempest*, with the function of both metaphor and metonymy, is the labyrinth. For the old Gonzalo, the island is "a maze trod indeed / Through forthrights and meanders" (3.3.2–3). For Alonso, king of Naples, all that has happened on this island "is as strange a maze as e'er men trod" (5.1.242).

In this synchronic reading of *The Tempest* the causal connections tend to loosen up and the plot becomes "a most strange story" (5.1.117); it begins "by accident most strange" (1.2.178), and ends as Ariel predicts with his song ("something rich and strange") by changing "from strange to stranger" (5.1.228). "Strange drowsiness" (2.1.194) overcomes the shipwrecked men and a "strange humming" (313) wakes them from sleep. They continuously hear "strange music" (3.3.17) or "moe diversity of sounds" (5.1.232), see "strange shapes" which "vanish strangely" (3.3.39); and they themselves are frozen within "this strange stare" (3.3.95). Alonso fears that Ferdinand was devoured by "a strange fish" (2.1.108). Trinculo considers Caliban "a strange fish." "Do not infest your mind with beating on / The strangeness of this business" (5.1.246–47). "The word 'strange' is constantly echoed through the play," writes Northrop Frye, "and Alonso opposes 'strange' to natural, to be told by Prospero that what he thinks strange actually is natural."[32] Alonso finds everything strange; Miranda finds everything new; only Prospero, who was cast out of Milan and who has spent twelve years on an uninhabited island with Ariel and Caliban, finds nothing strange or new.

"The isle is full of noises," says Caliban in the most penetrating of his lines (3.2.133). "Noises" are opposed to "voices." One hears voices and noises on the "uninhabited" island. As in dreams. "Sleep," "dreaming," and "waking" have, together with their grammatical derivatives, an amazingly high frequency: 49 of the 2062 lines of *The Tempest*. New relations of similarity, opposition, and transformation are revealed in a "musical" reading of recurring themes.

Miranda falls asleep and awakens onstage. Alonso and Gonzalo wake up onstage from their deep and almost fatal sleep. The mariners below deck were "dead of sleep." The murderers are joined by sleeplessness, and they recognize one another by their snoring: "This is a strange repose, to be asleep / With eyes wide open; standing, speaking, moving— / And yet so fast asleep." And in Sebastian's remark: "Thou dost snore distinctly; / There's meaning in thy snores" (2.1.207–9, 212–13). The temptation of the crown is a nightmare, which takes away sleep. ". . . and surely / It is a sleepy language, and thou speak'st / Out of thy sleep" (2.1.206–7). Antonio suddenly resembles Lady Macbeth.

Childhood memories return to Miranda like a fuzzy and forgotten dream. When for the first time Ferdinand sees Miranda, the boundaries between sleeping and wakefulness are blurred. "My spirits, as in a dream, are all bound up" (1.2.489). Caliban dreams that he is sleeping and awakens to a new dream:

> Sometimes a thousand twangling instruments
> Will hum about mine ears, and sometime voices
> That, if I then had wak'd after long sleep,
> Will make me sleep again; and then, in dreaming,
> The clouds methought would open and show riches
> Ready to drop upon me, that, when I wak'd,
> I cried to dream again.
>
> (3.2.135–41)

Graves's comment in *The White Goddess* is appealing: "the illogical sequence of tenses creates a perfect suspension of time."[33] In this time suspension, Ferdinand, who seemed a "spirit" and "god" to Miranda, is equated with Caliban: "To th' most of men this is a Caliban, / And they to him are angels" (1.2.483–84). In a parallel system of hierarchies, Miranda, who seemed to be a "goddess" to Ferdinand, is compared to a witch by Caliban: "I never saw a woman, / But only Sycorax, my dam and she; / But she far surpasseth Sycorax / As great'st does least" (3.2.99–101). In this system of relations Ferdinand, like Caliban, may seem a monster or an angel, and Miranda, analogously, a repulsive witch or a goddess. The relationship between Prospero, Caliban, and Miranda ("I had peopled else / This isle with Calibans" [1.2.352–53]) is reversed in the history of Alonso's daughter Clarabelle (almost an anagram for "Caliban") given in royal marriage to the king of Tunis against her will: "That would not bless our Europe with your daughter, / But rather lose her to an African" (2.1.120–21). This mediation between the Old and New Worlds through marriage will not repeat itself on "this most desolate isle."

This semantic code of repetitions, symmetry, inversion, and substitution is contained not only in the tense poetry of *The Tempest*; it is even more present in its theatrical vision. Actors and directors have frequently sought traditional "characters" in vain. *The Tempest*, like a fugue, has to be played according to its rigorous formal score.

Caliban's entrance at the beginning of scene 2 in act 2 with "a burden of wood" prefigures Ferdinand's entrance in the following scene of the next act (3.1) "bearing a log." Ferdinand on Prospero's plantation is in "wooden slavery" (62), transformed into a "logman" (67) like Caliban.

Shakespeare often plays the same tune in two keys. Yet the insistent, almost mechanical symmetry in the stories of Prospero, Ariel, and Caliban, and in unexpected equations of Caliban and Ferdinand, of Caliban and Miranda, contain something more than merely formal repetitions and echoes. The history is reduced to an elemental transition and exchange between the one who imprisons and the one who is imprisoned. This common and universal history is shown both in a realistic and mythic mode, in scenes from tragedy and from dell'arte, the opera seria and opera buffa, in the Old World and on the plantation of the New World.

The words "confine" and "release" mark the relation and opposition between prison and freedom. Ariel was imprisoned by Sycorax: "She did confine thee . . . into a cloven pine" (1.2.273–77). Caliban was imprisoned by Prospero: "Deservedly confin'd into this rock / Who hadst deserv'd more than a prison" (1.2.363–64). Alonso, Antonio, and Sebastian, "three men of sin," were in turn "confin'd together" (5.1.7). The royal retinue waits for Prospero to release them: "All prisoners, sir . . . they cannot budge till your release" (5.1.9, 11). He who has imprisoned them will free them: "Go release them, Ariel" (5.1.30). Ariel will also release three rebels at Prospero's behest: "Come hither, spirit: / Set Caliban and his companions free, / Untie the spell" (5.1.251–53).

Ariel, Sycorax's prisoner for twelve years and Prospero's slave for another twelve, an airy spirit and an airy jailer, who alternately imprisons and frees others, most desperately demands his own release:

PROSPERO: How now? moody?
    What is 't thou canst demand?
ARIEL: My liberty.
                                        (1.2.244–45)

Prospero promises liberty to Ariel seven times before setting him free in the last line of the play. For the sailors and the Boatswain, "liberty" means wakening from the "dead of sleep" (5.1.230–35). At first the prison where he sees Miranda once a day seems like liberty itself to Ferdinand: "all corners else o' th' earth / Let liberty make use of; space enough / Have I in such a prison" (1.2.494–96). (Fabrizio in Stendhal's *La Chartreuse de Parme* will repeat this almost literally when from the window of his prison he can see Clélia every day.) Once he experiences a slave's toil, he knows well that it is as difficult to endure as "to suffer: / The flesh-fly blow my mouth" (3.1.62–63). Prison is not liberty, any more; Ferdinand wants to unite with Miranda "with a heart as willing / As bondage e'er of freedom" (3.1.88–89).

There are also other, bitter and sardonic calls for "freedom." The usurper persuades the king's brother to gain his "freedom" through murder: "one stroke / Shall free thee from the tribute which thou payest: / And I the king shall love thee" (2.1.288–89). There are also Caliban's shouts at the end of his drunken song, when with Trinculo and Stephano he sets out to kill Prospero: "Freedom, high-day! high-day! freedom! freedom, high-day, freedom!" (2.2.186–87). Shakespeare's system of echoes is not confined to the *The Tempest*. Caliban's cries are an unexpected repetition of Brutus' words after the murder of Caesar: "Let's all cry 'Peace, freedom and liberty!'" (*Julius Caesar* 3.1.111). Cassius coldly interrupts Brutus: "Stoop then, and wash." Then he pauses, as if he had seen the murder from a distant time: "How many ages hence/ Shall this lofty scene be acted over / In states unborn and accents yet unknown!" (3.1.112–14). On this American plantation the drunken Caliban and the two pretenders to the title of viceroy rehearse once again the assassination of Caesar.

The past is the prologue in *The Tempest*, the future is the epilogue. Between the past and the future are three hours of *The Tempest*.

PROSPERO: What is the time o' the day?
ARIEL: Past the mid season.
PROSPERO: At least two glasses. The time 'twixt six and now
    Must by us both be spent most preciously.
                                            (1.2.239–41)

The performances in the Globe and in the public theaters began at two in the afternoon. The illusion of reality—as in Northrop Frye's succinct formula—becomes the reality of illusion.[34] In this theatrical time, which suddenly and unexpectedly becomes the time of spectators, the entire past in the play is both the history of the world and the past of the audience, from the journeys of Aeneas to the voyage to the Bermudas and Virginia. Prospero's future ("and time / Goes upright with his carriage") is the future of the audience, our own future and our own fate, chosen or imposed.

In the epilogue, in its sudden narrowing, as in the *stresso* of a fugue, all the themes return. But now the signs are literal. When the storm of the prologue ends, the scene changes into a "bare island." In the epilogue, when Prospero speaks directly to and perhaps even walks down into the audience, the island changes back into a bare stage.

> Now 'tis true
> I must be here confin'd by you,
> Or sent to Naples.
> (Epilogue, 3–5)

Once more the two key words, "confine" and "release," return, and between them the entire history of the world takes place. In the epilogue, Prospero is still a prisoner of the theater.

> But release me from my bands
> With the help of your good hands . . .
> (9–10)

The three hours in *The Tempest* are like the imaginary hours of Shakespearean comedies, a time of metamorphosis. When this time ends, the *dramatis personae* and spectators return to their ordinary world. "The action," writes Northrop Frye, "moves from appearance to reality, from image to substance. Once the real world is reached the mirage becomes nothingness." As in Prospero's bitter confession: ". . . the great globe itself, / Yea, all which it inherit, shall dissolve" (4.1.153–54).

In the well-known Renaissance treatise on architecture and the first after Vitruvius on the building of theaters Sebastiano Serlio writes: "Among all the things that may bee made by mens hands, thereby to yield admiration, pleasure to sight, and to content the fantasies of men, I thinke it is placing of a Scene, as it is sheved to your sight, where a man in a small place may see built by Carpenters or Masons, skillful in perspective worke, *great Palaces, large Temples, and divers Houses* . . ."[35] (my italics). Shakespeare's "cloud-capped towers, the gorgeous palaces, the solemn temples" (4.1.172) seem to echo the most famous passage of the newly (1611) translated Serlio's *Booke of Architecture*. But in this dramatic and rare confrontation of the two visions of the theater in Prospero's monologue the image of the city onstage with its great and superb buildings fades like an "insubstantial pageant" and "leave not a rack behind" (174–75).

The new art of perspective made it possible for the first time to build and paint onstage the wooden structure that gave the illusion of the Renaissance *città*. In the Palladio's Teatro Olimpico at Vicenza and in the later Gonzaga Theater at Sabbioneta, a spectator even today can see and admire a large proscenium like a *piazza* and a scene in three-point perspective representing five streets, as in Serlio's *Opere d'Archittetura*, "filled with Houses . . . tryumphant Arches, high Pillars or Columnes, Piramides, Obeliscens, and a thousand fayre things and buildings . . ." In the theater at Sabbioneta the large steps of the amphitheater rise to the elevated loggia with twelve columns crowned by the twelve Olympian gods. The Roman Olympians watch from the top of the theater like the Duke Vespasiano Gonzaga from his princely loggia the image of the Renaissance city built onstage.[36] The statues of the gods and image of the city are immovable. They both aspire to eternity. Onstage is preserved the unity of time and place and all hierarchies of rank and social order.

The "baseless fabric" of the Shakespearean stage is not the perspectival illusion of the real town. All places and all times can be present onstage in one instant. The fool accompanies the king and the royal son drinks with rogues and strumpets. "The great globe itself" is an emblem and a sign of *teatrum mundi*. The Globe, name and theater, image and building, stage and audience, two mirrors sending recipro-

cally their reflections, is the paradigm of the world and of
life. "All the world's a stage / And all the men and women
merely players" (*As You Like It* 2.7.140–41). "Potent Art,"
"rough magic," and "heavenly music" are the double of the
theater. The stage is a new purgatory in which everything is
repeated but nothing is purified.

> We are such stuff
> As dreams are made of; and our little life
> Is rounded with a sleep.
>   (4.1.156–58).

"*We*," in this most famous gnome of all *The Tempest*, are
the actors, who in Shakespeare's physics and the metaphysics
of the theater melt "into thin air" like spirits. A play ends in
oblivion. As does life. "Our revels now are ended" (4.2.167).
What remains is a bare stage on which the same tragedy/
comedy is replayed again and again.

Translated by Daniela Miedzyrzecka

Notes

1. See Howard Mumford Jones, *O Strange New World; American Culture:
The Formative Years* (New York: Viking, 1965), p. 31 and pl. IV, reproduction
of a painting by Mostaert; see also Hugh Honour, *The New Golden Land:
European Images of America from the Discoveries to the Present Time* (New York:
Random, Pantheon, 1975), pp. 22–24, pl. V.

2. *The Tempest*, ed. Frank Kermode, Arden Shakespeare (London: Methuen, 1975). All quotations are from this edition.

3. In Shakespeare's plays, Medea is invoked twice; in *The Merchant of
Venice*: "In such a night / Medea gathered the enchanted herbs / That did
renew old Aeson" (5.1.13–15) and in *King Henry the Sixth, Part II*, "Meet
I an infant of the house of York, / Into as many gobbets will I cut it / As
wild Medea young Absyrtus did" (5.1.57–59). Medea is the personification
of black magic. The incantations from Ovid's *Metamorphosis* are the main
source for Prospero's invocations of the spirits in 5.1.33–50.

4. See J. M. Nosworthy, "The Narrative Sources of *The Tempest*," *R.E.S.*
24 (1948): p. 290.

5. *The Aeneid of Virgil*, trans. Rolfe Humphries (New York, 1951). All
quotations are from this translation.

6. Silvester Jourdain, *A Discovery of the Bermudas* (1610), quoted in Kermode's notes to *The Tempest*, p. 141.

7. Honour, p. 8 and il. 1.

8. On Arcadia and the "Arcadian diet" see Erwin Panofsky, "Et in Arcadia
Ego," in *Meaning in the Visual Arts* (Garden City, N.Y.: Doubleday, 1955),
pp. 295–302; and Harry Levin, *The Myth of the Golden Age in the Renaissance*

(New York: Oxford University Press, 1969), p. 26. In another classical tradition of the savage Arcadia, also well known during the Renaissance, the Arcadians were called "acorn eating swine" (Philostratus, *Vita Apolonii* 7.7).

9.   Dryden, a translator of the *Aeneid*, adapted *The Tempest* to the new tastes of the Restoration and made it into a fantastic play. For him, Caliban was a mythic creature: "as from the distinct apprehension of a horse, and of man, imagination has formed a centaur; so, from these of an incubus and a sorceress, Shakespeare has produced his monster . . . he is the product of unnatural lust; and his language is as hobgoblin as his person; in all things he is distinguished from other mortals" (preface to *Troilus and Cressida*, 1679).

10.   Edmund Leach, *Genesis as Myth and Other Essays* (London: Cape, 1969), p. 11.

11.   This pertinent question was posed for the first time by D. G. James in *The Dream of Prospero* (Oxford: Clarendon, 1967), note on p. 108.

12.   ". . . his daughter and I will be king and queen . . . and Trinculo and thyself shall be viceroys" (3.2.104–6). A viceregal system of government was then the form of rule in the Spanish colonies.

13.   Jones (n. 1 above), p. 49: "The Anglo-Saxons remained alone in thinking that the only good Indian is a dead Indian."

14.   George Odell, *Shakespeare from Betterton to Irving* (1920; repr., New York: Scribner's, 1963), 2: 261.

15.   In Hooker's *History of Ireland* (1558). The verb "to colonise" was first used in English by Bacon in 1622 (Jones, p. 184).

16.   Another example of this unusual syntagmatic coexistence of two separate linguistic codes within a single line can be found in *Richard the Second*: "The king's grown bankrupt like a broken man" (2.1.257). An entire historical experience is in this "bankruptcy" of the lord's anointed.

17.   Around 1524, in a letter to Francis I, Verazzano called the shores of today's North Carolina an "Archadia," as they "reminded him of Arcady as described by Virgil or, more recently, Jacopo Sannazaro" (Honour, p. 16).

18.   As Jones puts it, "The golden age changed imperceptibly into an age of gold" (p. 34).

19.   For connections between the myth of paradisaic gardens and the golden age with the utopias of the new primitivism, see Charles L. Sanford, *The Quest for Paradise: Europe and the American Moral Imagination* (Urbana: University of Illinois Press, 1961), pp. 11–18.

20.   Richard Eden translated the first three books of *De orbe novo decades* (1530) into English and it was published in its entirety by M. Lok in 1612. For more about Shakespeare's acquaintance with Martyr, see Kermode, pp. XXXII–XXXIII, and James, op. cit., p. 81. For more about the myth of Paradise and the golden age in Martyr, see Jones, pp. 16–27, and Sanford, p. 57.

21.   See Erwin Panofsky, *Studies in Iconology* (New York: Harper & Row, 1972), p. 40: "There had been from the very beginning of classical speculation two contrasting opinions about the primeval life of man: The 'soft,'

or positivistic, primitivism as formulated by Hesiod depicted the primitive form of existence as a 'golden age,' in comparison with which the subsequent phases were nothing but successive stages of one prolonged fall from grace; whereas the 'hard,' or negativistic, primitivism imagined the primitive form of existence as a truly bestial stage from which mankind had fortunately escaped through technical and intellectual progress."

22.   Bruce Erlich compares this man-hunt for Caliban with Las Casas's descriptions of Spanish colonial cruelty (*Brévissima relación de las destrucción de las Indias*, 1540; the English translation dates from 1583): "The Spaniards train their fierce dogs to attack, kill and tear to pieces the Indians . . . They have Indians brought to them in chains, then unleash the dogs. The Indians come meekly down the roads and are killed" ("Shakespeare's Colonial Metaphor: On the Social Function of Theater in *The Tempest*; Seminar on Marxist Interpretations of Shakespeare," a paper read at the Second World Shakespeare Congress in Washington in April 1976).

23.   Jones, p. 70.

24.   Ficino writes the following on the trinity of time in his *De amore*: "I surmise, that God governs things by threes, and that the things themselves also are determined by threes . . . For the supreme maker first creates things, then seizes them, and thirdly perfects them . . . This was divined by Orpheus when he called Jupiter the beginning, the middle and the end of the universe: the beginning because he creates, the middle because he draws his creatures back to himself, the end because he perfects them as they return." Quoted by Edgar Wind, *Pagan Mysteries in the Renaissance* (New York: Norton, 1968), pp. 42–43. These passages from Ficino look very much like an allegorical and moral interpretation of *The Tempest*.

The first source of the Trinity of time was Plato (*Republic* 10): "there is another band, three in number . . . the Fates, daughters of Necessity . . . Lachesis singing of the past, Clotho of the present, Atropos of the future . . ." But the most direct of the sources of *The Tempest* was the appearance of the three Hours in person, in Ben Jonson's *Entertainment of the two Kings at Theobalds*, on July 24, 1606: "ouer the porch, sate the three Howers, upon clouds, as the ports of Heauen . . . of which, one bore a Sunnediall; the other a Clock; the third, an Hower-glasse . . ." (1–4).

25.   Thomas M. Greene, "The Norms of the Epic," *Comparative Literature* 13 (Summer 1961): 201.

26.   William S. Anderson, "Virgil's Second Iliad," *Transactions of the American Philological Association* 88 (1957): 17–30, shows how the signs and parallelisms of the *Iliad* have been inverted in the last six books of the *Aeneid*: Aeneas is identified with Achilles, the Trojans with the Greeks, Latinians with the Trojans, Turnus with Hector. The fall of Troy is symbolically inverted and repeated through Turnus' death. It is extremely characteristic that in mythic tradition, the Italians, French, and English have always identified with the Trojans and began their histories from the arrival of Aeneas and his companions, Frank and Brit, on their shores.

27.   Sanford (n. 19 above) says that "when the American colonists said that they were going to establish 'A City on a Hill,' they meant to found a sacred city and a new paradise." See also his chapter entitled "The Journey Pattern of Modern History," pp. 36–55.

28. Shakespeare uses an answering "echo" three times during Ariel's song leading Ferdinand along. The last "echo," "Cock a diddle dow," is characteristic (1.2.389). This struck Samuel Pepys, who saw the 1667 operatic adaptation of *The Tempest* and commented: "the most innocent play ever I saw; and a curious piece of musick in echo of half sentences, the echo repeating the former half, while the man goes on to the latter; which is mighty pretty."

29. The chess game often appears in illuminations beginning with the late Middle Ages. But it is always a royal couple or two princes that play. In *The Image of Christian Faith*, an early fifteenth-century drawing by Dirck van Delft of Utrecht, a king and queen play chess. Out of the black-and-white chessboard grows a large green tree. Probably it is a symbol of abundance and hope for a happy future for the royal family. At the bottom of this same initial, sons and daughters of the royal pair, all wearing crowns, sing. More dramatic is *The Chess Players* by Girolamo da Cremona from the second half of the fifteenth century, now at the Metropolitan Museum of Art in New York. The players are a young couple, both with fair hair skillfully dressed. They are both beautiful. Their game is near the end; only a few stones remain on the chessboard. The game is serious. Do they play for the future? We do not know. But three persons, a couple of friends behind the young man and another woman behind the maiden, look attentively at the chessboard. The girl player puts her hand on the hand of the young man. She does not look at the chessboard, she is pensive, almost far away with her thoughts. Is her future at stake? Behind the players is an open window, through which a pond can be seen and, further off, a park with trees.

30. Compare the dialogue between Hector, who fights according to knightly rules, and the cynical Troilus in *Troilus and Cressida*:

HECTOR: O, tis fair play.
TROILUS: Fool's play, by heavens, Hector.

(5.3.62)

31. The four "key words" spoken by Gonzalo are at the same time a description of the antimasque ("torment" and "trouble") and the masque ("wonder" and "amazement"). For the Renaissance Italian theoreticians from the latter half of the sixteenth century, such as Castavettro and Strozzi, "wonder" represented the essence of the new theater. Inigo Jones, who first introduced the "wonders" of Italian theatrical machines to England, was the great carpenter of masques and performances at Court. *The Tempest* was performed on the emblematic stage of the Globe without decoration. Apparently it was also performed at the Dominicans in the light of candles and torches. But even in the court theater, Blackfriars, scenographic "wonders" were not used. Prospero's vision of an "insubstantial pageant" which melts into thin air may be also a recollection of the theatrical wonders of Inigo Jones. A chronicler of the spectacles staged by Inigo Jones in Oxford in 1605, when he first used machines for scene changes, wrote: "in one of the spectacles new facades appeared on the whole stage with great variety and speed to the amazement of all" (*Rex Platonicus*, 1607). See Stephen Orgel and Roy Strong, *Inigo Jones: The Theatre of the Stuart Court* (Berkeley: University of California Press, 1973), pp. 4–7 and 823.

32.   Northrop Frye, *A Natural Perspective: Development of Shakespearean Comedy and Romance* (New York: Harcourt, Brace & World, 1965), p. 150.

33.   Robert Graves, *The White Goddess* (New York: Farrar, 1948), p. 427.

34.   Ibid., p. 116.

35.   *The First Booke of Architecture, made by Sebastian Serly, entreating of Geometrie. Translated out of Italian into Dutch, and out of Dutch into English. London Printed for Robert Peake.* Serlio's treatise first published in both Italian and French in 1545, was translated in the same year (1611) that *The Tempest* was first performed, but he was already known at the turn of the century. For a modern translation see *The Renaissance Stage: Documents of Serlio, Sabbattini and Furttenbach,* trans. Allardyce Nicoll, John H. McDowell, and George R. Kernodle (Florida, 1958), pp. 18–36.

36.   See Kurt W. Forster, "Stagecraft and Statecraft: The Architectural Integration of Public Life and Theatrical Spectacle in Scamozzi's Theater at Sabbionetta," *Oppositions* 9 (Summer 1979): 63–87.

The *Aeneid* and *The Tempest*

Within twenty-six lines, during their first conversation on Prospero's island, the shipwrecked men mention the "widower Aeneas" once and "widow Dido" no less than six times. This is striking in its redundance and, it would seem, stubborn insistence. It has always been a puzzle for the commentators. Frank Kermode remarks in a footnote to his edition of *The Tempest*: "This line begins a series of apparently trivial allusions to the theme of Dido and Aeneas which has never been properly explained," and adds, "It is a possible inference that our frame of reference is badly adjusted or incomplete and that an understanding of this passage will modify our image of the whole play."[1]

Later in the same scene Adrian and Gonzalo disagree as to whether Tunis was once Carthage. Alonso's sea route had led from Tunis to Naples (by way of Prospero's island): Aeneas had traveled from Carthage (Tunis) to Cumae (Naples) on the last leg of his journey, stopping at the west coast of Sicily where rites of purification were performed.

The insistent allusions to "widow Dido" seem to be what Roman Jakobson would call a "metalingual" sign, supplying the receiver with the code in which a message is to be encoded.[2] Shakespeare is telling us: "Remember the *Aeneid*." In the Elizabethan age and under the Stuarts the *Aeneid* was read in the schools and was an obligatory exercise for translation. Shakespeare undoubtedly read it while a schoolboy, and he surely had the Latin text at hand while writing *The Winter's Tale*.[3] During the sixteenth century the *Aeneid* was translated into English four times, and Shakespeare may well have been familiar with its English versions.[4]

But the *Aeneid* existed not only as a text and its successive translations. Not unlike the Bible it shaped the cultural and literary consciousness of the West for centuries. It was at the same time text and *lectio*, from the allegorical interpretations of the Middle Ages to Neoplatonic hermeneutics and the Renaissance myth of the New World. This *lectio*, or the Virgilian code (as I am going to call it), provided the paradigm of a journey by sea understood both as Everyman's journey through penance into salvation and as the discovery of the Promised Land.

To what extent is the *Aeneid* the key, or one of the keys, to *The Tempest*? Does Shakespeare repeat and at the same time negate the Virgilian myths of purification of men and history through suffering and of civilizations lost and rewon?[5] The answers lie not only in the analogies, echoes, and borrowings from the text of the *Aeneid*, but in the continuation and transformation in *The Tempest* of the theatrical use of classical icons in the pastorali, interludes, and masques.

The *Aeneid* is not the "source" of *The Tempest* in the narrow philological sense. Traditional philology is insufficient when the epic is transformed not merely into drama but into spectacle. The three scenes in which the impact of the *Aeneid* is most pronounced—the tempest of the prologue, the interrupted banquet, and the wedding masque—are also the most spectacular of the play.

Both Virgil's epic and Shakespeare's play begin with a tempest, artificial and providential, created, directed, and calmed with the help of supernatural agents. The spectacular "overture" of the play begins with *crebris micat ignibus aether* (*Aen.* 1.90[6] "The skyis oft lychtnyt with fyry levin / And Schortly bath ayr, sey and hevin" [trans. Douglas 1.2.65–66]),[7] transformed into the first stage directions: *"[On a ship at sea]: a tempestuous noise of thunder and lightning heard"* (1.1.1). Virgil's *crebris micat ignibus aether* reappears in Ariel's account: "I flamed amazement: sometime I'd divide / And burn in many places" (1.2.198–99). These lines also imply suggestions for the actor's performance, if indeed Ariel is to appear in person in the first scene.[8] And perhaps it is worth recalling that commentators have compared the flashes on the topmast with St. Elmo's Fire, which frightened navigators sailing the tropical seas. The Italian sailors, still living within the classical traditions, called it St. Hermes' Fire.[9]

Shakespeare did not have to search through classical literature or contemporary travel accounts to describe a storm at sea. More significant than the borrowed classical motifs, such as "Jove's lightning" (1.2.201) or the "dread trident" (1.2.206) of Neptune, is the way Shakespeare adopts the actual scenario of *Aeneid* 1. The royal ship sinks with its entire crew and then is somehow safely led to harbor; the rest of the fleet is dispersed and later united with the king's ship; the hero swims ashore to find his fellow travelers alive and healthy. In *Aeneid* 1 Venus tells Aeneas (399–400):

> haud aliter puppesque tuae pubesque tuorum
> aut portum tenet aut pleno subit ostia uelo.

In Douglas's translation:

> Thy schippys and falloschip on the sammyn wyss
> Owdir ar herbryit in the havyn, I wyss
> Or with bent saill entris in the port be this.
>   (1.6.158–60)

And almost in these very words Ariel reports to Prospero that his command has been carried out: "Safely in harbour / Is the King's ship; in the deep nook . . . and for the rest o' th' fleet, / Which I dispers'd, they all have met again" (1.2.226–27, 232–33).

The dramatic resolution of the shipwreck scene is also borrowed from *Aeneid* 1.[10] Venus, Jove's daughter, stands sadly by her mighty father and they both gaze down from the heavens into the rolling seas:

> Smylyng sum deil, the fader of goddis and men,
> With that ilk sweit vissage, as we ken,
> That mesys tempestis and makis the hevynnys cleir,
> First kyssit his child, syne said on this maneir:
> "Away sik dreid, Cytherea, be nocht efferd.
> For thi lynage onchangit remanys the werd."
>   (Douglas, 1.5.47–52)

In Virgil this passage ends (257–58):

'parce metu, Cytherea, manent immota tuorum
fata tibi . . .'

And Shakespeare follows closely:

Be collected;
No more amazement: tell your piteous heart
There's no harm done.

(1.2.13–14)

The theatrical working-out of this scene on the heights of
Olympus is even more interesting than Shakespeare's verbal
allusions. Miranda, as we know from her dialogue with her
father, watched the sinking of the ship. The logic of the stage
dictates that both Prospero and Miranda observed it from
the upper gallery. Similarly, Prospero would carefully observe
the scene of the interrupted banquet. Prospero is, of course,
invisible to the "three men of sin" but not to the audience.
In the English stage tradition followed until the end of the
nineteenth century Prospero and Miranda descend to the
platform at the start of the second scene. Now the stage
becomes an island, the whole house the sea, as in this contemporary description of a performance at the Fortune
playhouse:

The very floor, as't were, waves to and fro
And, like a floating island, seems to move
Upon a sea bound in with the shores above.[11]

In *Aeneid* 4 Mercury, the divine messenger, carries Jove's
command to Aeneas. On his way down to the sea he disperses
the winds and forces his way through the clouds; *illa fretus
agit uentos et turbida tranat / nubila* 4.245–46). Surrey's translation (1557) reads:

By power wherof he driues the windes away
And passeth eke amid the troubled cloudes.

(4.316–17)[12]

Ariel's lines echo Virgil's Mercury: "To fly, / To swim, to dive
into the fire, to ride / On the curl'd clouds" (1.2.190–92).
Virgil's Mercury is obedient to Jove ("When Ioue had sayd
/ Then Mercurie gan bend him to obey / His mightie fathers

will" [Surrey, 4.307–9]) as Ariel is obedient to Prospero ("Hast thou, spirit, / Perform'd to point the tempest that I bade thee?" [1.2.193–94]). Mercury, having accomplished his task, disappears from the sight of mortals and vanishes into the air, as does Ariel complying with Prospero's command:

> When Mercury had said
> Amid his tale far of from mortall eies
> Into light aire, he vanisht out of sight.
> (Surrey, 4.356–57)

The Neoplatonic doctrine of the trinity of animus, anima, and matter might be helpful in illuminating the theology of Ariel as spirit. But for an understanding of the theatrical nature of Ariel and his action onstage we have to go back to the epic. Gods and their messengers in Homer and Virgil are only seen by the mortals to whom they choose to speak, and they change disguises as Ariel does in *The Tempest*. This epic convention is transformed into the optics of the theater. Ariel, the "divine messenger," must be at the same time visible and invisible onstage.

Panofsky and his school examined with clarity and precision the double exchange between classical themes and their meanings in the late Middle Ages and Renaissance. In the first type of exchange the classical icons of gods and heroes are invested with a new meaning without changing their representations or signs. The Roman Hercules carrying an Erymanthian boar on his shoulders was transformed into an allegory of Christ in a fifteenth-century bas-relief in St. Mark's in Venice. The figure of Atlas was understood as St. John the Evangelist. In the second type of exchange the actions, characters, and situations are repeated, but their icons are modified to suit the medieval requirements.[13] In the *Trojan Cycles* Helen, Andromache, and Cassandra are shown standing on a gallery watching the tournaments of knights with the gloves of their ladies pinned to their helmets. An illumination from an early medieval manuscript depicts Aeneas and Dido as a regal couple playing chess in the manner of Ferdinand and Miranda at the end of *The Tempest*. A late fifth-century manuscript represents Iris with wings and a halo, holding a rainbow in her hands, floating down to Turnus (*Aen.* 9.2) who awaits her in medieval armor and a helmet adorned with a plume. In the same manuscript a marvellous illustration presents the storm (*Aen.* 1.888ff) with deadly floods and a shipwreck under a darkened sky. The terrified Aeneas stands in the middle of a ship desperately raising both hands to heaven. The image could easily be taken for an illustration of Antonio in the prologue to *The Tempest,* rather than Aeneas. Except that in the dark sky above the ship where Ariel was "to fly,/to swim, to dive into the fire/1.2.190–91), the artist shows Juno holding two fire-spitting torches and the personifications of the Winds.[14]

The first type of exchange may be called a *transcriptio,* the second type a *translatio.* The transformation of classical signs is important not only in the images of late medieval romance but even more for plot and setting of Renaissance poetry and drama. In a late thirteenth-century manuscript Thisbe and Pyramus converse through the opening in a column supporting two Gothic arches; in the next scene Thisbe awaits Pyramus sitting on a Gothic tombstone of King Ninus. A harmless looking lion sniffs at a nearby tree growing on Pyramus' grave.[15] As in *The most Lamentable Comedy, and most Cruel Death of Pyramus and Thisbe,* the lion has just arrived "to bury the dead" (*A Midsummer Night's Dream* 5.1.348). The setting and action in the performance staged by Peter Quince and his troupe of Athenian mechanicals are surprisingly similar to the Pyramus and Thisbe of these medieval illuminations.

The image of Puck, a strange combination of the classical satyr with Robin Goodfellow from English folklore (see illustration on the cover), did not at all resemble the Renaissance Cupid. Yet Puck's malicious mistakes exactly repeat the folly of "blind Cupid." Ariel, even more than Puck, derives from the classical icons inherited and transformed by the Renaissance. He rode on the "curl'd clouds" (1.2.192) like Virgil's Mercury who "circled away, / With misty cloudes" (4.321–22). This Mercury, "skimmer of the clouds," became for the Neoplatonists an essential and frequently evoked symbolic sign. He was the master of spirits, mediator between gods and men, sky and earth. Mercury in Virgil is the one who *lumina morte resignat* (4.244).

He calles from hell pale gostes: and other some
Thether also he sendeth comfortlesse.
Wherby he forceth sleepes, and them bereues,
And mortal eies he closeth vp in deth.
(Surrey, 4.312–15)

For Boccaccio, in his *De genealogia deorum*, as well as for
Ficino, Mercury was the one who carried and revealed the
hermetic mysteries.[16] The symbol of this knowledge was his
caduceus, his "wande" (Surrey, 4.311). Like this caduceus
carried by Hermes-Mercury, Prospero's wand is an indis-
pensable instrument of his magic. In the late medieval tradition Mercury is also the protector of the benevolent sorcerers
and the patron of musicians. Like quicksilver to which he
lent his name he can assume any imaginable shape. The
Neoplatonists called him the divine mystagogue, since he
disperses not only real clouds but the clouds which dim and
darken the human mind.

The charm dissolves apace;
And as the morning steals upon the night,
Melting the darkness, so their rising senses
Begin to chase the ignorant fumes that mantle
Their clearer reason.
(5.1.64–68)

Ariel, in the manner of the Neoplatonic Mercury, takes away
the sinners' senses "when no man was his own" (5.1.213) and
then restores them.

In *Aeneid* 6 the souls in purgatory undergo purification
by fire, water, and wind.[17] The *psychopompos* or *interpretor se-
cretorum*, as Boccaccio calls Mercury, is, in *The Tempest*, the
agent of this purification and punishment.

In the Italian intermezzi of the late sixteenth century,
Mercury is the mythical figure who appears most frequently.
In *La Pellegrina*, performed in Florence in 1589, he is shown
in the company of the gods with a winged caduceus and large
wings grown from his abundant locks. The Paris *Ballet Co-
mique de la Reine* (1581), which became famous at all the courts
as a new style of entertainment, had a great impact on the
Stuart masque. In it Mercury and Minerva save Odysseus
from Circe's charms. Mercury descends from the clouds accompanied by thunderclaps. The Renaissance Mercury is

represented in sixteenth-century engravings and woodcuts as a beautiful nude youth with a mantle thrown over his left shoulder. Small tattered wings grow from his head and his feet, and in his hand he holds a caduceus.[18]

Mercury first appears in England at the end of the fifteenth century in the Digby plays of St. Paul in the role of a demon's accomplice. But with the Renaissance Mercury suddenly embarks upon a new career as an entertainer and "presenter," as in the pageants in honor of Anne Boleyn and later in the "excellent princely masque" performed for Queen Elizabeth at Norwich (1578).[19] By 1600 Mercury was so familiar and popular in the theater that Jonson in his Induction to *Cynthia's Revels* says: "By the way, *Cupid* meets with *Mercurie*, (as that's a thing to be noted, take anie of our play-bookes without a *Cupid*, or a *Mercurie* in it, and burne it for an heretique in *Poetrie*.)"[20] In Stuart masques Mercury is a divine messenger, patron of the sciences and the exorcist of cosmic vice. He appears in them at least eleven times, including three times before the date of *The Tempest*.[21]

Jonson's early *Entertainment of the King and Queen at Theobalds* contains all the elements of the magic theater of *The Tempest*:

> And withall, the black vanishing, was discouered a glorious place . . . in which were placed diuers Diaphanall glasses, fill'd with seuerall waters, that show'd like so many stones, of orient and transparent hiewes. Within, as farder off, in Landtschap, were seene clouds riding, and in one corner, a boy figuring *Good Euent*, attyred in white, houering in the ayre, with wings displayed, hauing nothing seene to sustaine him by, all the time the Shew lasted: At the other corner, a Mercurie descended, in a flying posture, with his *Caduceus* in his hand, who spake to the three *Parcae* . . . the third . . . with a booke of Adamant lying open before them. But first, the *Genius* surpriz'd by wonder urg'd this doubt, by question.[22]

Here, for the first time, Mercury is accompanied by the "airy-spirit." This winged boy, Good Euent, seems to be the theatrical prototype of Ariel. Perhaps, also, this "booke of Adamant" was transformed into the magical books of the magus Prospero. Jonson scrupulously annotated his early masques explaining the classical sources of his emblems or, as he called them, "Hieroglyphickes." In *Hymenaei* the veil of Juno is trimmed with "Fascia, of seuerall-coloured silkes" (218). Jonson supplied "Fascia" with a note:

> After the manner of the antique *Bend*, the varied colours implying the seuerall mutations of the *Ayre*, as showres, dewes, serenitie, force of winds, clouds, tempest, snow, haile, lightning, thunder, all which had their noises signified in her Timbrell: the facultie of causing these, being ascribed to her by *Virg. Aeneid. lib.* 4 where he makes her say, *his ego nigrantem commixta grandine nimbum Desuper infundam, et tonitru coelum omne ciebo.*
>
> (217, n. to 218)

Hymenaei was published in quarto and performed at the beginning of 1606. The theatrical image of "Ariel, an airy spirit" and all its transformations are already found in Jonson's note.[23] In the play Juno is accompanied by the "spirites of the ayre, in seuerall-colours, making musique" (223–24), the predecessors of the winged boy from *Entertainment at Theobalds.*[24]

From then on the "Airy spirits" are often seen in the Stuart masques. In Campion's *Lord Hay's Masque* (1607) Zephyrus is costumed "in a mantle of white silk propped with wire, still waving behind him as he moved . . ."[25] In Samuel Daniel's *Tethys Festival* (1610), one year before *The Tempest,* Zephyrus enters "in a short robe of greene satin imbrodered with golden flowers, with a round wing made of lawnes on wyers, and hung down in labels. Behind his shoulders two siluer wings. On his head a Garland of flowers consisting of all colours" (*311*, 70–75).[26] The emblems of the air-spirit: wings and the rainbow ("seueral-colours"; "sky-coloured taffeta"; "all colours") are always repeated. Shakespearean Ariel wore a rainbow-colored tunic and wings.[27]

When at Prospero's command Ariel transforms himself into a "nymph o' th' sea," "invisible / To every eyeball else" (1.2.303–4) he probably threw about him a transparent "robe for to goo invisibell."[28] He did not have much time to change his costume: only twelve lines separate Ariel's exit from his return to the stage looking "like a water-nymph" (stage direction, 1.2.318).

Ariel is next transformed into a Harpy. Sea nymphs and Harpies are related in mythology, but the interrupted banquet derives directly from *Aeneid* 3. When Aeneas and his companions landed on the shore of the Strophades which, like Prospero's island, "man doth not inhabit" (3.3.57), they were attacked by Harpies who snatched away their supper.

> Quhen suddanly, with horribill dyn and beir,
> From the montanys the harpeis on vs fell
> With huge fard of weyngis and mony a yell.
> Our mesis and our mete thai reft away . . .
> (Douglas, 3.4.32–35)

These Virgilian birds, with their crooked talons and girls' faces, were well preserved in Shakespeare's memory: "with thine angel's face . . . with thine eagle's talons" (*Pericles* 4.3.46–48).[29] This "angel's face" had for Shakespeare a theatrical relevance. Ariel as a Harpy did not have to alter his boyish face. In his disguise he would be easily recognized by the audience.

"*Thunder and lightning, Enter ARIEL like a Harpy; claps his wings upon the table*" (stage direction, 3.3.52). This most detailed stage direction was already known as a translation from Virgil at the end of the eighteenth century. The mythical birds were associated with guilt and punishment. But Shakespeare borrowed from the *Aeneid* more than the Harpies' attack with "dyn and beir . . . on the altaris" of the invaders. The episode on the Strophades also contains a prophesy. Celaeno, a "dreary prophetess," announces to Aeneas and his companies:

> ibitis Italiam portusque intrare licebit.
> sed non ante datam cingetis moenibus urbem
> quam uos dira fames nostraeque iniuria caedis
> ambesas subigat malis absumere mensas.
> (3.254–57)

In Douglas's rendering:

> To Itale sal ye wend, and thar tak land.
> Bot first, or wallis of the cite vpstand
> Quhilk by the goddis is you predestinate,
> For strang hungir sal ye stand in sik state,
> In wraik of our iniuris and bestis slane,

That with your chaftis to gnaw ye salbe fane,
And runge your tabillis . . .

(3.4.87–93)

When Ariel covers the table with his big Harpy's wings, "with a quaint device, the banquet vanishes" (stage direction, 3.3.52). The table probably stood on a trap door, and the plates were quickly removed by a stage hand. Later, when he raises his wings, the table is bare.[30]

When Aeneas and his companions arrived at Latium their hunger drove them to eat so ravenously that Aeneas' son said jokingly, "We are eating the very tables!" (*etiam mensas consumimus* [7.116]). The "three men of sin" in *The Tempest* almost chew their very tables out of hunger.

The "quaint device," often used in the Italian intermezzi and later in the *opera buffa*, was never used in any other of Shakespeare's plays. In this brilliant employment of theatrical magic Celaeno's prophecy was at the same time made visible and changed into a spectacle of strangeness.

Later in the same scene Ariel, repeating Celaeno's harangue, turns the "innocent Harpies" expelled from their "rightful realm" (*patrio Harpyias insontis pellere regno*, 3.249) into Prospero and his innocent daughter driven from Milan.

But remember—
For that's my business to you—that you three
From Milan did supplant good Prospero;
Expos'd unto the sea, which hath requit it,
Him and his innocent child . . .

(3.3.68–72)

In the double prophecy of winged Celaeno hunger and torment precede the founding of a city at Latium. The harsh sermon given by Ariel the Harpy to the "three men of sin" contains also a double prophecy, of penance and forgiveness: "in this most desolate isle . . . is nothing but heart-sorrow / And a clear life ensuing" (3.3.80–82). After the attack by the Harpies and Celaeno's prophecy, the Virgilian "sinners" turn numb with fright: *at sociis subita gelidus formidine sanguis / deriguit* (3.259–60).

The suddane dreid so stonyst our feris than,
Thar blude congelit and al togiddir ran;

> Dolf wolx thar spretis, thar hie curage down fell,
> No mair thame lykis assayng sik batell.
>
> (Douglas, 3.4.95–98)

Gonzalo, the "true preserver" (5.1.69), possesses the righteousness and unshaken faith of Anchises. After the attack by the Harpies, Aeneas' father did not lose heart, but called to the gods for mercy:

> et pater Anchises passis de litore palmis
> numina magna uocat meritosque indicit honores:
> 'di, prohibete minas; di, talem auertite casum
> et placidi seruate pios.'
>
> (3.263–66)

In Douglas's rendering:

> Bot our fader, hevand vp his handis,
> The gret goddis dyd call, and on the sandis
> Hallowis thar mycht with detful reverens:
> "O hie goddis, forbyd syk violens,
> Stanch this bost and ondo this myscheif,
> Salve petuus folkis, ameyss your wrath and greif."
>
> (3.4.103–8)

Gonzalo also walks away from his companions after the fearful moment and raises his hands in prayer. There is a truly Virgilian ring to his lines:

> All torment, trouble, wonder and amazement
> Inhabits here: some heavenly power guide us
> Out of this fearful country!
>
> (5.1.104–6)

When the Harpies snatch away the food, Aeneas and his companions reach for their swords and raise them to strike at the birds, "Bot thar was na dynt mycht thar fedderis scheir, / Nor in thar bodeis wound ressave thai nane" (Douglas, 3.4.66–67). When "Alonso, Sebastian, etc., draw their swords" (stage direction, 3.3.60) and raise them against Ariel the Harpy and his "fellow ministers," the swords, as in the *Aeneid*, freeze in their bearers' hands:[31]

> the elements,
> Of whom your swords are temper'd, may as well
> Wound the loud winds, or with bemock'd-at stabs
> Kill the still-closing waters, as diminish

One dowle that's in my plume: my fellow-ministers
Are like invulnerable.
                                              (3.3.61–66)

Invulnerable monsters and hybrids are once again met by
Aeneas during his descent to the Land of the Dead: "Thar
beyn eik monstreis of mony diuerss sort: / The Centawres
war stablit at this port, ... / The laithly Harpyes, and the
Gorgones thre" (Douglas, 6.4.101–2, 108). Aeneas had already drawn his sword when "his expert mait Scybilla / Tawcht
him thai war bot voyd gaistis all tha, / But ony bodeis, as
wandrand wrenchys waist" (Douglas, 6.4.115–17).

> et ni docta comes tenuis sine corpore uitas
> admoneat uolitare caua sub imagine formae,
> inruat et frustra ferro diuerberet umbras.
>   (6.292–94)

The theatrical sign of the monsters' invulnerability is the
raised sword magically stopped in mid-air. In *The Tempest* the
Harpies' magic is evoked thrice and each time the swords are
prevented from touching the enemy. The sword of Ferdinand, pointed at Prospero, "is charmed from moving" (stage
direction, 1.2.469); the swords of Sebastian and Antonio raised
above sleeping Alonso are stopped by Ariel's music; and the
swords of the "three men of sin" freeze in their hands as they
strike at the Harpies.

The third transformation of Ariel, after the sea nymph
and Harpy, occurs in the masque. Ariel prepared the masque
on Prospero's command and took part in it himself. He played
the role of Iris who introduced the goddesses and presented
Ceres (4.1.167).[32] He did not have to change his "tunic of silk
in rainbow colours."[33] Iris' costume was always rainbow-hued.[34]
In the masque of *The Tempest* she is a "wat'ry arch," presented
exactly as Iris is in an illumination in Vergilius Romanus.
Ceres greets her as a "many-coloured messenger" (4.1.76)
and calls her a "heavenly bow" (86). Through his transformations from his first appearence Ariel is always winged. Of
the three goddesses in the masque only Iris had wings. The
attire of gods and goddesses is always emblematic in the Stuart
masques. Before Juno's entrance Iris sees her "peacocks . . .
fly amain" (74). In Daniel's *Vision of the Twelve Goddesses* (1604)

Juno enters "in a sky-colour mantle embroidered with gold and figured with peacocks' feathers" (*189*, 82–83); Ceres appears "in straw colours . . . with ears of corne and a dressing of the same" (*191*, 129–31).

The "most majestic vision, and / Harmonious charmingly" (4.1.118–19) which Prospero conjures up for Ferdinand and Miranda on the uninhabited island seems to repeat all the conventions of court wedding masques. One cannot but be surprised that Venus and the "blind Cupid" are absent from these mythological revels; in Jonson's masques alone Cupids appear at least twelve times. The mischievous boy with his inevitable bow and quiver was transformed from "blind" to "seeing," and his divine mother promised to watch him strictly in the future. Venus and Cupid appear in Jonson's *The Haddington Masque* (1608), which defends the sanctity of marriage. Jonson's note tells the story of the unhappy union of Dido and Aeneas, in which the culprit was Cupid. At his mother's command, in the shape of Ascanius, he stealthily pricked Dido with his arrow. Iris' explanation of the absence of Venus and Cupid in the masque of *The Tempest* is either an allusion to the *Aeneid* as in Jonson or simply a *locus classicus*.

> Here thought they to have done
> Some wanton charm upon this man and maid,
> Whose vows are, that no bed-right shall be paid
> Till Hymen's torch be lighted: but in vain;
> Mars's hot minion is return'd again;
> Her waspish-headed son has broke his arrows,
> Swears he will shoot no more.
>
> (4.1.94–100)

There are even more classical reminiscences derived arguably from the *Aeneid*[35] or the Renaissance textbooks of iconology. During the Vitruvian revival the mythological setting became an obligatory convention in the Stuart masque. What is unexpected is the violent interruption of the Feast of Harvest in *The Tempest*; this is contrary to all the conventions of the wedding masque which invariably ended with the presentation of gifts to the young couple and a festive choral epithalamium. The dramatic rupture of Prospero's revels recalls the scene in *Aeneid*—disruption of the hunt preparing us for the wedding pageantry of Dido and Aeneas.

> In the meane while the skies gan rumble sore:
> In tayle therof, a mingled showr with hayle.
> The Tyrian folk, and eke the Troyans youth,
> And Venus nephew the cotage for feare
> Sought round about: the floods fell from the hils.
> . . .
> And Iuno that hath charge of mariage,
> First tokens gaue with burning gledes of flame,
> And priuie to the wedlock lightning skies.
> (Surrey, 4.206–10, 213–15)

Hymen's torches go out in the pouring rain; the nymphs, scattered in confusion, cry out from the heights: *fulsere ignes et conscius aether / conubiis summoque ulularunt uertice Nymphae* (4.167–68). "And the Nymphes yelled from the mountains top" (Surrey, 4.216).

In his disruption of the betrothal masque Shakespeare retained Virgil's dramatic tension and the shock of interruption. Prospero's masque ends suddenly even before the gifts of the harvest are presented to the young couple. As in the tempest and the attack by the Harpies the narrative has been transformed into spectacle. Here the impact of the *Aeneid* can be discovered for a third time through the stage directions: "*Enter certain Reapers properly habited; they join with the Nymphs in a graceful dance: towards the end whereof Prospero starts suddenly, and speaks: after which, to a strange, hollow and confused noise, they heavily vanish*" (stage direction, 4.1.138).

In the *Eneados* of Douglas the Virgilian origin of this "strange, hollow and confused noise" (*Interea magno misceri murmure caelum / incipit* [4.160–161]) is even more emphatic:

> In the meyn quhile, the hevynnys al about
> With fellon noyss gan to rummyll and rowt.
> (4.4.63–64)

"Our revels now are ended" (4.1.148). When the masque is interrupted, "our actors . . . are melted into air" (4.1.148–50). The act ends with cruelty and despair.[36] In Prospero's moving confession the entire world faded into nothingness,

like an "insubstantial pageant." For the first and last time
Prospero admits defeat—his art fails him, nature proves
stronger than nurture: "all lost, quite lost . . . I will plague
them all, / Even to roaring" (4.1.190, 192–93).

For Dido disaster follows the terrifying sound from the
sky,[37] "Ay me, this was the first day of their mirth, / And of
their harmes the first occasion eke" (Surrey, 4.217–18). Darkness at high noon foreshadows a tragedy: the suicide of the
Queen of Carthage and renunciation of personal happiness
by "pious" Aeneas. Prospero, "sent to Naples" (*Ep.*, 5), departs from his "most desolate isle" like Aeneas, obedient to
his fate ("Against my will to Italy I go" [Surrey, 4.471]).

This bitter finale of the wedding masque is one of the
most unusual evocations of the Virgilian code. *The Tempest*
repeats the sequence of the first four books of the *Aeneid*:
the sinking of the royal ship, the saving of the shipwrecked
men, the attack by the Harpies, the ordeal of hunger and
thirst, the interrupted wedding pageantry. The Virgilian code
becomes the theater of Prospero's art.

> The direful spectacle of the wrack, which touch'd
> The very virtue of compassion in thee,
> I have with such provision in mine Art
> So safely ordered . . .
>
> (1.2.26–29)

Prospero's art is referred to ten times—on five of these
occasions "art" means the theatrical art which Prospero em-
ploys to stage his Virgilian drama on the "uninhabited island": "If by your Art, my dearest father, you have / Put the
wild waters in this roar . . ." (1.2.1–2). Shakespeare emphasized from the beginning the theatricality of Prospero's magic.
Prospero himself calls the masque "Some vanity of mine Art"
(4.1.41). The illusion of the reality of events is soon destroyed: "Spirits, which by mine Art / I have from their con-
fines call'd to enact / My present fancies" (4.1.120–22). In
Prospero's revels the "meaner fellows" (4.1.35), the "rabble"
(4.1.37) play the parts of spirits. The Virgilian "strange shapes"
are only "living drollery" (3.3.21) for Sebastian.

It is a theater-within-a-theater which Prospero prepares:
its principal actor is Ariel.

The time 'twixt six and now
Must by us both be spent most preciously.
(1.2.240–41)

Prospero talks to Ariel like a theater director to his as-
sistant, warning him not to waste time. The time was short,
just three hours, no longer than the spectacles at the Globe.
"Ariel, thy charge / Exactly is perform'd: but there's more
work" (1.2.237–38).

The word "perform" occurs seven times in *The Tempest*—
of these four refer to Ariel's enacting the parts in the three
"Virgilian" scenes: "Hast thou, spirit, / Perform'd to point
the tempest that I bade thee?" (1.2.193–94). And again when
Ariel is duly praised following the interrupted banquet:
"Bravely the figure of this Harpy hast thou / Perform'd, my
Ariel" (3.3.83–84). And for the last time when Ariel is about
to prepare "a most majestic vision": "Thou and thy meaner
fellows your last service / Did worthily perform; and I must
use you / In such another trick" (4.1.35–37). The snatching
of the food by Ariel the Harpy is only a theatrical trick:
another such trick consists of his inciting the "goddesses" to
quick motion (4.1.39). Ariel is a "tricksy spirit." "Trick" also
had a precise and concrete theatrical meaning: it was used
"to denote an elaborate device or ingenious piece of mechanism used for pageantry."[38] The concept of *ostranenie*, de-
familiarization, introduced by the Russian formalists, and
later used with such great brilliance by Brecht, could best
describe the artifice of a "second theater" in *The Tempest* deliberately baring its own devices.[39] The storm and the ship's
sinking are neither realistic nor imaginary but theatrical. The
theater of Prospero's magic is really the theater of Ariel's
performance: at first Ariel's only audience is Prospero and
Miranda who witness the sinking of the ship; then Prospero
himself, "invisible," at the scene of the interrupted banquet;
and finally, Prospero and the young couple at the masque.

Shakespeare had employed once before a similar strategy
of *ostranenie* in the presentation of the theater-within-a-theater in *A Midsummer Night's Dream*. The theater of mechanicals
with its carefully revealed devices is performed twice in re-
hearsals even before the wedding ceremony at which *The most*

Lamentable Comedy, and most Cruel Death of Pyramus and Thisbe is to be performed. But the "second theater" of carpenter Peter Quince is a pre-Shakespearean theater, derived from mummings, folk-game plays, drolls, and disguisings.[40] Ariel's is, however, a new theater whose great "Carpenter" was none other than Inigo Jones.

In this new theater the clouds rise, as in *Entertainment at Theobalds*, and Mercury descends "in a flying posture with his Caduceus in his hand" (155, 37–38). In Jonson's *The Masque of Blackness* (1605) an "artificiall sea" was "seen to shoote forthin selfe abroad the room."[41] In his *Masque of Beauty* (1608) when "a curtaine was drawne" an island appeared "floting on a calme water" (186, 164). In *Tethys Festival* again the scene was "a Port or Hauen" with "many Ships, smal and great, seeming to be at Anchor, some nearer, and some further off, according to prospective" and "in a moment the whole face of it was changed, the Port vanished, and Tethys with her Nymphes appeared in the seuerall Cauerns gloriously adorned" (*311*, 58–62; *315*, 195–97).

The tempest and sinking were staged at the Globe and even at court with the old devices of the Elizabethan stage, but Shakespeare, the producer and man of the theater, probably also designed his last play for the possibilities of a new stage whose marvels could suddenly change a prospect of a ship sinking into "The Island: Before Prospero's Cell."

On Prospero's island the Virgilian motifs are shown through songs, dances, and "wonders" of the old theatrical magic. Between the *Aeneid* and the *Aeneid* in *The Tempest* there intervenes a long and rich theatrical tradition of the use of classical icons in the court spectacles. The sources of Shakespeare's classical allusions from the treatises of the Renaissance iconographers, like Giraldi and Cartari, have been carefully investigated. An important new field of research, following the example of the Warburg school, could trace the *transcriptio* of these icons into court spectacles. The theatrical signs of *The Tempest* were however not shaped by the Stuart masque alone.[42] The introduction of the Virgilian code here is also inspired by the emerging theatrical form of *dramma per musica.*

For this historian of theater the sixteenth-century court ballet in France and the seventeenth-century English masque are Baroque theater. For the music historian the Italian intermezzi, French ballet, and the Stuart masque are the sources of opera. Count Bardi and the Florentine Camerata believed Greek tragedy was originally sung and danced, and the French and Italian humanists, poets, and musicians dreamed of a theater in which Greek tragedy would again be brought to life in the union of words, music, and dance. To this end the *musica nova* with the recitative and aria was well adapted, but theatrically what was required was the discovery of an essentially lyrical hero whose tragedy could be sung in the new *stilo recitativo* with musical accompaniment.

Sophocles' *Oedipus Rex* was performed in 1585 in Vicenza with splendid scenery and sung choruses. Yet this incestuous Oedipus who gouged out his own eyes was the hero of a court spectacle only once. Throughout the late sixteenth century the Italian pastorali were set in Arcadia with shepherds and shepherdesses visited by Mercury in the company of satyrs and nymphs. But the hero of the *dramma per musica*, in the same Arcadia, tames the wild beasts with song and the strumming of his lute—Orpheus, the divine singer and lutenist, was to be the first hero of the opera.[43]

In Monteverdi's *Orfeo* (1607) Orpheus decends to Hades to recover his wife Eurydice. To gain entrance he must first put the ferryman Charon asleep, as Aeneas (in *Aeneid* 6) would have to render the fierce Cerberus harmless; Orpheus' trick, however, is not Aeneas' "morsel charged with drowsiness": music is his magic. He descends to Hades with an aria, each strophe of which is accompanied by a different ensemble of instruments. "Charon's slumber," writes D. J. Grout, "is depicted by the strings with organ of wood pipes, playing very softly and the same organ alone accompanies Orpheus' song as he crosses the river Styx . . ."[44] The "divine singer," like Virgil's Mercury, "gives sleep and takes it away," *dat somnos adimitque* (4.244).

Monteverdi's *Orfeo* was likely to have been the most important theatrical event of Shakespeare's lifetime. It was widely known among poets and musicians. "Slumber scenes," lulling to sleep by music and song, became common in opera through the end of the seventeenth century. In *The Tempest* the inducing of sleep and of sudden awakenings is the very essence of Prospero's art and Ariel, the musical spirit, is the executor and agent in this "mortal business" (1.2.409). Miranda, Alonso, and Gonzalo sleep and waken under magic spells. Alonso, after the "interrupted banquet," hears the "deep and dreadful organ pipe" (3.3.98) which along with the sound of stringed instruments had lulled Charon to sleep in *Orfeo*. "Where should this music be? I' th' air or the 'arth?" (1.2.390). Ferdinand is led about the island following the music of Ariel's two arias, "Come unto these yellow sands," and "Full fadom five" with its echo repeating four times as in the echo-song in *Orfeo*.[45]

The *Aeneid* in *The Tempest* is both a paradigm and a spectacle. But in this paradigm the New World is not the Promised Land; the purification is ambiguous and Prospero, unlike Aeneas, returns to his native dukedom. The Virgilian myths are invoked, challenged, and finally rejected. The "second theater" in *The Tempest*, the three scenes from the *Aeneid*, are enacted as wonders, masque, and *dramma per musica*. But the wonders are theatrical "tricks," the masque is disrupted and the *dramma per musica* is the saddest in the history of opera. Ariel's "second theater," "the delight of princes," will melt into air like the "insubstantial pageant."

When, during the Restoration, *The Tempest* returned to the stage in balletic and operatic adaptations only one of the two theaters remained. The whole play was now Ariel's theater, but it was now a different Ariel. In 1611 at Court, Ariel was probably played by the "principal boy" of the Children of the Queen Majesty's Revels. On the Restoration stage Ariel was played by a female soprano singer in a low-cut dress, with flowers in her long hair, and was joined by a "spirit mate, Milcha," with whom she could sing duets. The imaginary scenery of the mythical island of the Old World and the plantation of the New one was rendered with dark mountains, cypresses, citrus groves, caves, and grottoes of some fantastic Capri. All the old "miracles" of the theatrical art were employed in this new *Tempest* at the theater in Dorset Garden:

The front of the Stage is open'd and the Band of twenty-
four Violins, with the Harpsicals and Theorbos which accompany the Voices are plac'd between the Pit and the Stage. While
the Overture is playing, the Curtaine rises and discovers a
new Frontispiece joined to the great Pilasters, on each side of
the stage. This Frontispiece is a noble Arch, supported by
large wreathed Columns of the *Corinthian* Order; the wrea-
thing of the Columns are beautifi'd with Roses wound round
them, and several *Cupids* flying about them. . . .
Behind this is the Scene, which represents a thick Cloudy
Sky, a very Rocky Coast, and a Tempestuous Sea in perpetual
Agitation. This Tempest (suppos'd to be rais'd by Magick) has
many dreadful objects in it, as several Spirits in horrid shapes
flying down amidst the Sailers, then rising and crossing in the
Air. And when the Ship is sinking, the whole House is darken'd and a shower of Fire falls upon 'em.[46]

But the Virgilian code by now was incomprehensible and
was disregarded. Prospero's island no longer lay on Aeneas'
sea route between Carthage and Cumae, nor near the Bermudas. The "uninhabited island" became the "Enchanted
Island," as *The Tempest* was renamed in the 1667 production.
Ariel was no longer Hermes the psychopompos, Mercury the
trickster, or Orpheus the divine musician. The Virgilian Harpies at the interrupted banquet were replaced by a "dance
of fantastick spirits." The shipwrecked men on Prospero's
island no longer mention the "widow Dido" or the "widower
Aeneas."[47] The Virgilian code was buried for centuries and
did not reappear in the theater even when the play was performed with its original text in 1838.

Translated by Daniela Miedzyrzecka

Notes

1.   *The Tempest*, ed. Frank Kermode, Arden Shakespeare, 6th ed. (London,
1975), note to 2.1.74. All quotations are from this edition.

2.   Roman Jakobson, "Linguistics and Poetics" in *Style in Language*, ed.
Thomas Sebeck (Cambridge, Mass., 1960), pp. 355–56.

3.   "Shakespeare's Isle of Delphes," T. J. B. Spencer, *Modern Language Review* 47 (1952): 201–2. Outside of *The Tempest* Shakespeare mentions Dido
eight times in seven plays. The most significant lines which recall the *Aeneid*
(6.450 ff.) are from *The Merchant of Venice*: "In such a night / Stood Dido
with a willow in her hand / Upon the wild sea-banks and waft her love /
To come again to Carthage" (5.1.9–12). Outside of *Troilus and Cressida*
and *The Tempest*, Aeneas is mentioned nine times in eight plays. In *Julius
Caesar* (1.2.112–14) Cassius speaks of Aeneas carrying his father Anchises

out of Troy upon his own shoulders. Similarly in *Henry VI*, Pt. 2: "But then Aeneas bare a living load" (5.2.64) (Spevack's *Concordance*).

4.   Gavin Douglas's *Eneados* was published in 1553, but manuscripts were widely circulated earlier. The translation by Surrey of the second and fourth books of the *Aeneid* appeared in 1557. Seven books of the *Aeneid*, translated by Thomas Phaer, were published in 1558. The post-mortem edition of Phaer's translation (1562) contains nine books and the beginning of the tenth. The last translation that Shakespeare could have been familiar with was *The First Fore Books of Virgil* by Richard Stanyhurst, 1582. The *Eneados* is the greatest masterpiece of English translation in the sixteenth century. From a stylistic viewpoint, Surrey's translation appears closest to *The Tempest*. I quote the *Aeneid* 2 and 4 in Surrey's version, the remaining books in Douglas's.

5.   Kermode writes in his introduction to *The Tempest*: "*The Tempest* also bears the marks of application of an old learning to a new world. Its strong echoes of the *Aeneid* . . . reflect the philosophical attitude of the Old World to the New" (p. xxxiv). See also notes to verses 1.2.377, 424; 2.1.74, 78; 3.3.52 (stage direction), 66; 4.1.78, 102. The most exhaustive analysis of the connections and borrowings between the *Aeneid* and *The Tempest* thus far is contained in a controversial work by Colin Still, *The Timeless Theme: A Critical Theory Formulated and Applied* (London, 1936), and in J. M. Nosworthy, "The Narrative Sources of *The Tempest*," *R.E.S.* 24 (1948): 287–94. Still was perhaps the first to stress the analogy between Aeneas' journey and the sea route of Alonso, and to point out the echoes of the *Aeneid* 4 in *The Tempest*. For him, however, the play is merely an allegory of a purification rite. Nosworthy examines the *Aeneid* as a traditional source of plots and characters. Ferdinand represents Aeneas in the first part of the play. The value of this small paper was long underestimated, especially its detailed analysis of the opening storm and shipwreck scene in Virgil and Shakespeare. Cf. also Tucker Brooke, *The Works of Christopher Marlowe* (London, 1910), *Dido, Queen of Carthage*, note to 1.1.235–37, and Northrop Frye, *A Natural Perspective: The Development of Shakespearean Comedy and Drama* (New York, 1965), p. 156. Geoffrey Bullough, in his *Narrative and Dramatic Sources of Shakespeare* (New York, 1975), does not list the *Aeneid* among the sources of *The Tempest*.

6.   *P. Vergili Maronis Opera*, ed. R. A. Mynors (Oxford, 1969). All Latin quotations are from this edition.

7.   Gavin Douglas, Bishop of Dunkeld, *Virgil's Aeneid Translated into Scottish Verse*, ed. D. F. C. Coldwell, 4 vols. (Edinburgh: Scottish Text Society, 1957–64).

8.   In *The Tempest* directed by Kean at the Princess Theatre in 1857 Ariel appeared in the first scene of the play suspended on ropes above a ship on fire. See C. D. Odell, *Shakespeare from Betterton to Irving* (New York, 1963), vol. 2, plate on p. 346.

9.   See Kermode, op. cit., p. 142 and E. M. Butler, *Ritual Magic* (London, 1949), p. 168.

10.   See Nosworthy, op. cit., p. 291.

11.   In *The Roaring Girl*, by Middleton and Dekker, quoted from A. M. Nagler, *Shakespeare's Stage* (New Haven and London, 1958), p. 107.

12. *The Aeneid of Henry Howard Earl of Surrey*, ed. with an introduction and notes by Florence H. Ridley (Berkeley and Los Angeles, 1963).

13. Erwin Panofsky, *Studies in Iconology, Humanistic Themes in the Art of the Renaissance* (1939; rpt., New York, 1967), pp. 18–20.

14. Illuminations of the *Virgilius Romanus* (Cod. Vat.: Lat. 3867), fol. 74v. and fol. 77r. See Erwin Rosenthal, *The Illuminations of the Vergilius Romanus* (Zurich, 1972), pp. 43–44 and 52–53. See also Kurt Weitzmann, *Late Antique and Early Christian Book Illumination* (New York, 1977).

15. Reproduction from *Studies in Iconology*, pl. Va.

16. See Edgar Wind, *Pagan Mysteries in the Renaissance* (New York, 1967), pp. 100, 121 ff., 196; Jean Seznec, *The Survival of the Pagan Gods: The Mythological Tradition and Its Place in Renaissance Humanism and Art* (New York, 1961; French ed. 1940), pp. 17, 22, 180 ff., 254. See also Still on the relation of Ariel to Hermes, op. cit., pp. 222–23.

17. *Aeneid* 6.740 f.

18. Panofsky, *Meaning in the Visual Arts* (New York, 1955), pp. 273–74 and illustrations 71–74; also Frances A. Yates, *The Art of Memory* (Chicago, 1966). On an engraving from 1555, a figure wearing a hat, holding in his hand instead of a caduceus a seven-branched golden candlestick, represents Mercurius Trismegistus (p. 170 and illustration on the frontispiece). These images of Mercury-Ariel may prove salutary to modern directors, who thus far have found his representation so puzzling; one production even had Ariel appear as an astronaut.

19. Paul Reyher, *Les Masques Anglais* (Paris, 1909; rpt., New York, 1964), pp. 389–90; John C. Meagher, *Method and Meaning in Jonson's Masques* (Notre Dame, 1966), p. 5.

20. Ben Jonson, *Works*, ed. C. H. Herford and Percy and Evelyn Simpson (Oxford, 1925–52), 4:36, 45–49.

21. Jonson's *The Entertainment at Highgate* (1604) and *The Entertainment at Theobalds* (1607), and Daniel's *Tethys Festival* (1610). In Inigo Jones's drawings for Jonson's masques, *Pleasure Reconcild to Virtue* (1618) and *The Masque of Augurs* (1622), Mercury is shown in a loose transparent coat worn over his naked body, with a feathered hat and the inevitable caduceus (Stephen Orgel and Roy Strong, *Inigo Jones: The Theater of the Stuart Court* [Berkeley, 1973] illustrations 93 and 118, pp. 293 and 342–43.) See also Allardyce Nicoll, *Stuart Masques and the Renaissance Stage* (New York, 1938), pp. 180 and 186.

22. Jonson, op. cit., 7:*155*, 26–43; all further Jonson quotations with page and line references are from this volume.

23. Jonson took the description of the transformations of *Ayre* from the *Iconology* by Ripa (Rome, 1593, and the following editions), one of the authorities on Renaissance mythography. Yet Ripa in turn repeats the old tradition of the commentaries on the *Aeneid* starting with Martianus Capella. See Jonson, 10: Commentary, *473* and Allan H. Gilbert, *The Symbolic Persons in the Masques of Ben Jonson* (New York, 1965), pp. 150–51. In his note Jonson quotes two lines from the *Aeneid* 4. 120, 122. In Surrey's translation: "A cloudie showr mingled with haile I shall / Poure down, and then with thunder shake the skies" (4.154–55). Bullough, op. cit., reprinted

fragments of *Hymenaei* as a "possible source" of *The Tempest*, but omitted all of Jonson's notes.

24. Cf. Enid Welsford, *The Court Masque* (1927; rpt., New York, 1962), p. 336: "Shakespeare, when he conceived Ariel, had in mind those musicians who in Ben Jonson's masque *Hymenaei* were seated upon the rainbow 'figuring airy spirits, their habits various, and resembling the several colours caused in their part of the air by reflection,' chief among whom was the famous Alphonso Farrabosco, 'a man planted by himself in that divine sphere, and mastering all the spirits of music.' "

25. Quoted after Gilbert, op. cit., p. 258.

26. *The Complete Works in Verse and Prose of Samuel Daniel*, ed. Alexander B. Grosart (London, 1885), 4 vols. All quotations from Daniel's masques, with page and line references, are from this edition.

27. Ernest Law, in *Shakespeare's Tempest as originally produced at Court* (London, 1920), p. 20, was the first to reconstruct Ariel's costume "from Inigo Jones' sketch . . . of a costume for an 'Aery Spirit' in some play or masque, and from Ben Jonson's description of a very similar costume for 'Jophiel, an *Airy Spirit*,' in his masque of *The Fortunate Isles* acted in 1626." Jones's drawing was designed for this masque of Jonson's. See Nicoll, op. cit., fig. 116, p. 159 and *Festival Designs by Inigo Jones* (International Exhibition Foundation, 1967), illustration 47. The costumes of air spirits did not undergo change during the first twenty years of the Stuart masque; "Iophiel, an aery spirit, and (according to the *Magi*) the *Intelligence of Iupiters* sphere" is similarly "attired in light silks of seuerall colours, with wings of the same, a bright yellow haire, a chaplet of flowers, blew silk stockings, and pumps, and gloues, with a siluer fan in his hand" (707, 3–7). See Stephen Orgel and Roy Strong, *Inigo Jones: The Theater of the Stuart Court* (Berkeley: University of California Press, 1973), reproduction of costumes. "This is a good instance of the discrepancy between Jonson's textual description of costume and Jones's actual designs. Jophiel, the Airy Spirit, has no chaplet of flowers on his head, nor silver fan on his hand" (p. 379).

28. Kermode, note to 1.2.303.

29. Quoted by Kermode in his note to *The Tempest* 3.3.52.

30. See J. C. Adams, *The Globe Playhouse* (Cambridge, Mass., 1942), pp. 319–22, and Kermode, op. cit., pp. 154–55.

31. See Kermode, notes to 3.3.65, 66.

32. See Kermode, note to 4.1.167: "presented" means "acted" or "introduced," as in "presenter of the masque." Irwin Smith, in "Ariel as Ceres," *Shakespeare Quarterly* 9 (1958): 430–32, argues rather unconvincingly that Ariel had enough time to change his costume between appearances. Ariel is recognizable precisely because of his wings. Shakespeare is remarkably consistent about his theatrical vision. In stage direction 4.1.124, *"Juno and Ceres whisper and send Iris on employment."* Ariel too was always sent "on employment." For Ariel as Iris see also R. A. Foakes, *Shakespeare: The Dark Comedies to the Last Plays* (Charlottesville, 1971), pp. 159–60.

33. Ariel is a "divine messenger" like Mercury and Iris. In medieval illuminations to the *Aeneid* (see above) Iris like Mercury descended from the clouds with a scarf "in seuerall colours" thrown about his shoulders. The tradition which has Mercury lower himself from heaven on a rainbow

reaches back to the second century, when Philostratus gave his Mercury a rainbow-colored chlamys in his *Imagines* (I.10). Renaissance iconology assigned the emblems of the rainbow to the Zephyrs who help Mercury to descend to Aeneas: *nate, uoca Zephyros* (*Aeneid* 4.223). In Surrey's translation: "call to thee windes. / Slides with thy plumes" (4.285–86). Thus Ariel owes to Virgil even his rainbow-colored attire.

34.   In Samuel Daniel's *The Vision of the Twelve Goddesses* (1604) Iris, the presenter of goddesses, is "decked like a Rainebow" (op. cit., 3:*198*, 41). In Jonson's *The King's Entertainment in passing to his Coronation* (1603) Iris "hasts to throw / Her roseat wings, in compasse of a bow" (*107*, 708–9); in *Hymenaei* she appears beneath Juno as a "rainbowe" (*217*, 226). In Beaumont's *The Masque of the Inner Temple and Gray's Inn* (1613) Iris is "apparelled in a robe of discoloured taffeta figured in variable colours, like the rainbow, a cloudy wreath on her, and tresses" (*A Book of Masques* [Cambridge, 1967], p. 134, 89–90).

35.   Iris's "saffron wings" (4.1.78) and Juno's movements ("I know her by her gait" [102]) are derived from *croceis . . . pennis* (4.700) and *uera incessu patuit dea* (1.405). This is one of the earliest discovered textual borrowings from Virgil.

36.   If the masque was indeed added later to the second court performance to add splendor to the court wedding, as was suggested by H. D. Gray (*Studies in Philology*, vol. 18 [1921]), then it would have had to be placed at the end of the play with an epithalamium, as in *A Midsummer Night's Dream*. A conventional wedding masque could not end with the "confused noise" and the disruption of pageantry.

37.   A parallel musical effect of a "confused, rumbling sound in the sky" was used by Chekhov in *The Cherry Orchard*: "Suddenly a distant sound is heard, as if from the sky, like the sound of a snapped string mournfully dying away" (Chekhov, *The Major Plays*, trans. Ann Dunnigan [New York, 1964], p. 347).

38.   Welsford, op. cit., p. 124, and Kermode, note to 4.1.37.

39.   See Fredric Jameson, *The Prison House of Language* (Princeton, 1972), pp. 75–79.

40.   Glynne Wickham, *Early English Stage 1300 to 1660* (New York, 1963), 1:191 ff.; 2:2, 32–34.

41.   Quoted from Nicoll, op. cit., p. 58. About the sea scenes in the masques see Nicoll, pp. 58–59, 62–63, 84–85. See also Jonson, 7: Commentary, 408–11.

42.   Since Welsford's book (1927), which was crucial for its investigations of the masque, critical literature on the Stuart masque and its impact on contemporary plays has been abundant. Among most recent works see Inga-Stina Ewbank, " 'These pretty devices,' A Study of Masque in Plays" in *A Book of Masques*, op. cit., pp. 407–48 and a bibliography on Jonson's masque in Meagher, op. cit., pp. 187–88. And one of the most recent collections is *The Court Masque*, ed. David Lindley (Manchester: Manchester Univ. Press, 1985). The most important is always the monumental Orgel and Strong *Inigo Jones*.

43.   The earliest pastoral play was Poliziano's *Orfeo* performed sometime between 1472 and 1483 at Mantua, with songs and one chorus. The earliest

opera, whose music survives, based on the Orpheus theme was *Euridice* performed in 1600 at Florence. The opera ends with Euridice leaving Hades. Aside from Peri's and Caccini's opera about Orpheus, and Gluck's and Haydn's *Orfeo ed Euridice*, music dictionaries enumerate nearly half a hundred operas about Orpheus.

44. Donald Jay Grout, *A Short History of Opera* (New York and London, 1947), p. 53.

45. Of the eleven stage directions in *The Tempest* for the orchestra in the Court "Musick Howse" or in the Globe's music gallery, nine are suggestions for Ariel's performance: "confused," "strange" or "hollow" noises; "soft," "sweet," or "solemn" music. On echosong in *Orfeo* see Grout, op. cit., p. 20. On music of *The Tempest* at Court, see Law, op. cit.: ". . . 'The Musick-Howse' by the stage, in which were stationed the King's band of some thirty or forty musicians," p. 16. "Soft" and "heavenly" music was probably played by lutes, harpsichords, and violins, as in Campion's *Lord Hay's Masque* (1607); "loud" music of "strange" and "confused" noises was played by the firm bass of a trombone and the bowed instruments. See Edward J. Dent, *Foundations of English Opera* (New York, 1965), pp. 21–33; see also Jonson, op. cit., 10: Commentary, *500*.

46. *The Tempest Or, The Enchanted Island*. A Comedy: As it is now Acted, by His Majesties Servants (London, printed for F. Tonson and T. Bennet, 1701). Other editions: 1674, 1676, 1690, 1692, 1695, 1710, 1733, and with Kemble's additions, 1793. All of these printed Dryden's preface, dated December 1, 1669.

    The Tempest returned to the stage in Dryden's and D'Avenant's version in 1667. After 1674 it was performed in Shadwell's version, and after 1695 with Purcell's music.

47. Nearly a quarter of a century before *The Tempest* was written *Aeneid* 4 was dramatized by Marlowe in *The Tragedie of Dido*. In 1689 Purcell wrote the music to Nahum Tate's libretto *Dido and Aeneas*. This chamber opera is today considered to be the masterpiece of seventeenth-century English music. Yet, aside from Dido's suicide, not much was left in it from the *Aeneid*. Aeneas is cheated by witches who, out of hatred for Dido, order one of the spirits to assume the shape of Mercury. See Dent, op. cit., pp. 178–96. The Renaissance Virgilian code was already lost to opera.

Appendix

Prospero, or The Director

Right in front of the footlights stands "invisible" Prospero, back to the audience, watching the magic table covered by the enormous wings of Ariel-Harpia. While a terrified Alonso and the would-be regicides leave in panic, Ariel appears on stage. In his hand he is holding Harpia's apparel. He cocks his head, drops a curtsy, smiles, awaiting praise. "Bravely . . . hast thou perform'd my Ariel," Prospero cries from the audience. At the final rehearsal before opening night, Giorgio Strehler repeated that scene seven times. He pushed Prospero aside; none of his gestures seemed to him sufficiently expressive. Twice Strehler ran to congratulate Ariel and shake hands with him. The entire episode was only to elaborate a single line of Shakespeare's text. On that night before the opening I saw two *Tempests*, one on the stage, where Prospero puts all the wonders and all the terrors of his theatrical magic into motion, and the other in the audience, where the last duke of Piccolò Teatro di Milano usurped the part of Prospero. Strehler directed that *Tempest* with his back to the stage and to his actors; in the enormous, still empty theater he was playing a magus to his first audience: his fellow-critics and a handful of friends. "*Impossibile*," he was shouting, "if I manage to show half of *The Tempest* it will be a *miracolo*." But which half? Prospero's magic or the failure of it? The vanity and the power of an almighty director able to will the elements to obey him, or a bitter renunciation of an Art capable of recreating all of the world's history but having no power to change it?

The frontispiece to Rowe's edition of *The Tempest* (1709) shows a three-masted frigate, its sails folded, being struck by huge waves. Zigzags of lightning shoot across a sky covered with dark clouds. Over the ship, whose stern is plunging into the sea, floats a tiny figure with open wings, holding a torch. Ariel was carried above the sinking ship as a ballerina hanging from a wire. After the Restoration and up until the mid-eighteenth century, *The Tempest* was staged as opera-ballet. Prospero's island, where the drama of the Old and the New World is played out, became a fairy-land. In Dryden's and Kemble's adaptations the tragic themes of *The Tempest* were already lost: but for the first time there was discovered and presented a magic fairy-land which Shakespeare could not produce either in the empty "O" of the "Globe" or even on the courtly stage at Blackfriars. There are two theaters in *The Tempest*, the old theater of emblems and the new stage of illusion which Inigo Jones carried over from Italian pastorale to the Stuart masque. *The Tempest* is the most Italian of all Shakespeare's plays, not only in plot, in the names of its characters, in the Milan and the Naples which he evokes. *The Tempest* is Italian in its amazing evocation of the *Aeneid*. But the most Italian aspect of *The Tempest* is its theatrical fabric, from Ariel's recitativo, Stephano's and Trinculo's *lazzi*, repeated after the *dell'arte* scenarios, to the Roman goddesses to the betrothal masque. Giorgio Strehler had decided to bring the English *Tempest* back to its Italian lineage: Prospero was to return to Milan for the second time.

In the prologue, a huge transparent canvas drops down and billows out. A frigate with open sails is visible through the cloth. Sailors climb up the lines trying to save their lives. The mast breaks. The deck collapses into the waves. It was the most spectacular theatrical storm I have ever seen. But theatrical inventions are almost always the repetition of tradition. Strehler's spectacular storm was performed almost precisely in accordance with a well-known recipe which had been described in a mid-sixteenth-century treatise on theater. The orchestra pit was divided into three corridors, with its floor shaped into mounds and hollows. "Operators" hidden inside the corridors walked up and down the mounds and hollows, pulling behind them blue ribbons which rose and fell like waves of a stormy sea. The baroque *macchina* was moved by human hands. Strehler's first plan was to make the "machine" visible. Later he decided not to show it. Only at rehearsal—and this was one of the most beautiful "theatrical moments"—did I see for a fleeting instant the boys and girls carrying the blue sea on their raised arms.

The director of *The Tempest* did not disclose his art, yet he did not conceal his power. When in the second scene the frightened Miranda rushes in, crying over the drowning people, Prospero gathers her to himself, putting his left arm around her. In his right hand he holds a rod with which he slowly calms the waves. Prospero's staff, the wand of Mercury, was changed to an opera conductor's baton; the book of magic spells from the Renaissance library is a director's copy from the theater library.

The stage is an island, and the island is a stage. Prospero's island is a platform built of wooden boards nailed together, surrounded on two sides by the sea. Luciano Damiani's scenography is astonishing in its simplicity, consisting of a few elements, all of them rich as theatrical emblems. The wooden deck which, when cut in half and placed at a slant, becomes "another place" on the island, is at the same time a raft on the sea and a platform of a popular theater stage. In the center it is covered with sand. The magic circle is the zodiac outlined in the sand. Prospero, in a white outfit apparently made of sailcloth, has an embroidered kerchief thrown over his shoulders. As soon as the magic incantation is over, the father and daughter shall fold it into eighths, just like the sheets, hurriedly taken out of the house, which Goneril and Regan also folded into eighths and threw into baskets in Strehler's *Re Lear*. The raft-stage is also a props room. Miranda will lift the wooden lid and she will place the magic cloth in the chest hidden inside the platform. Prospero will take Ariel's costumes out of another chest inside the island-props room.

Ariel is lowered by the cable down from the opera stage "heavens." He falls in the sand, turns over on his back, rolls on the ground. Then he floats up again, glides through the air like a circus acrobat and disappears; only his legs, rapidly walking through the air, can be seen under the upper frame of the proscenium. He comes down again to sit on Prospero's shoulders. Ariel is not a spirit: in Prospero's theater "actors . . . were all spirits." Ariel's "substance"—and here is one of the discoveries of the Milan *Tempest*—is his theatrical body. Ariel's "humanness" is his theatrical profession. In a white tunic and white, flowing trousers, neither boyish nor girlish, having only a theatrical gender, Ariel is a Pierrot out of Watteau imprisoned on Prospero's island. Giulia Lazzarini has Pierrot's sad, sometimes ironical little face powdered with flour.

Ariel is obedient; he will play any role and is proud of his skill and his travesties. But at the same time he is scared to death of his acting. He yearns for freedom, and when Strehler-Prospero delays the moment of his liberation, he tugs at the theatrical cable to which he is tied as to a chain. The prop suddenly becomes a metaphor and a sign. In this surprising theatrical psychomachy, a master-slave bond is converted into a director-actor relationship. Strehler is, furthermore, a prisoner of his imagination, of this theater and of all the plays he has ever directed. In his *Tempest* Ariel is sometimes transformed into the Fool from his *Re Lear*. In Strehler's production the Fool and Cordelia were played by the same actress. The Ariel of his *Tempest* is a "theatrical" daughter of Prospero. He has more affection for Ariel than for Miranda. I do not blame him.

The theatrical interpretation of the text is a discovery of the proper signs. The sign of the magic stroke was always for me the sword suspended in the air. Strehler interpreted the text better: "If you could hurt,/Your swords are now too massy for your strengths,/And will not be uplifted." When Ferdinand swings the sword at Prospero, Ariel pushes it down to the ground with one little finger and buries its blade in the sand. Shakespeare's Ariel lulls the new arrivals to sleep with his singing, as Orpheus lulled Charon to sleep in Monteverdi's opera. For Strehler, the singing was not enough; he tried to give it a visibility. His Ariel lulls the castaways to sleep by throwing the sand in turn into the eyes of Gonzalo, Alonso, and his court. And there are other theatrical inventions. Ariel is first transformed into a "nymph o' th'sea." I had never before quite understood the purpose of this disguise, since Ariel was to be "invisible." Strehler's Ariel-Nymph reels Ferdinand in on a fishing rod from the depths of the orchestra pit.

An opening in the center of the platform-island, covered with a wooden lid, makes up Caliban's cave. Before letting Caliban out of the cave, Prospero takes off his wide leather belt. The belt is a sign of the power of a planter in colonies of the New World. Slowly a pair of black hands rise out of the cave and take hold of the frame at the opening. With difficulty Caliban pulls himself up onto the platform-island. There is a strap around his hips, his hair has fallen over his eyes. He is a black slave who might, except for his fear of the leather belt, attack his master. Yet when Miranda steps out from behind Prospero, suddenly the face of Caliban changes. For an instant he is a desperately sad, almost timid boy. He has brushed his disheveled hair back from his face: against the background of a glowing horizon, on the bright, sand-covered island, he is a beautiful black youth.

There is one other brief moment in the Milan *Tempest* when a lyrical flow of poetry engulfs the stage and suddenly seems to permeate the figure of Caliban. Shakespeare gave Caliban a staggering line: "The isle is full of noises." Ariel's music in the Milan *Tempest* is played on medieval instruments. Caliban hears the music and he hears Ariel's song. In the scene with the drunkards he will suddenly repeat Ariel's song. These are the only two instances in the play in which Shakespeare's Caliban—awakening from his dreams only to dream again, the "noble savage" of the Renaissance philosophers and the rebellious slave of *The Tempest*'s colonial metaphor—has not been trivialized.

Summoned forth in *The Tempest* are all the types of theaters that Shakespeare knew, from the Plautine comedy about two slaves—the clever and the lazy—to the baroque illusionary stage of the myth enacted. But they are never resuscitated for the sake of show. They are repeated like a counterpoint in music, once in a lyrical key and later in buffo. In two scenes with the buffoons, "this thing of darkness," born by a witch from the devil, is transformed into a comical monster from *lazzi* of *dell'arte*. But even in this grotesque transformation, the themes of tragedy return: Caliban swears upon a bottle of sack to be the true subject of a drunken butler, and kisses a bottle as though it were the Bible. Shakespeare is never afraid of great parable. On the island of the New World, two drunkards and a slave from the plantation set out to kill a tyrant. In this violent dramaturgy, the *dell'arte* scenario suddenly becomes a political tragicomedy. On the desert island, the drunken feast of rebellion is in progress.

Traditionally, Caliban has almost always had a kind of proto-human, animal-fish appearance. Strehler places across his shoulders the skin of a sea reptile with stuffed skull and fins. That totem-skin is to be a remnant of the times when Caliban was the king of the island or a tribal chief. Strehler unfortunately succumbed to the temptation of primitivism or "strangeness" in a quasi-"anthropological" and now-fashionable version. For this Caliban he added to the Shakespeare text, or rather "staged in," some African or voodoo rituals and made him hop around in a ceremonial war dance. This artistically wrong stylization contradicts the Renaissance vision.

Trinculo is the Neapolitan Pulcinella, Stephano the Capitano from *dell'arte*. In Milan's *Tempest*, the *lazzi* grow into a long and wearying intermedium of a dumb savage and two drunkards of whom Ariel, transformed suddenly into a clown, makes fun. In the Shakespearean *Tempest*, Caliban's rebellion was not foreseen and is the most awesome failure of Prospero's education. Prospero never sent Ariel to accompany the drunken lazzi. The "tricks" of Ariel playing on a tabor and pipe are merely the music which unsettles and warns. Shakespeare's Prospero is a director of limited resources who never abuses his power. Ariel is used by him for most important tasks. Strehler is a director who never has enough of the feast of the spectacle.

When the magic table disappears, Ariel—the she-bat with claws and enormous black wings—glides in and out of the ceiling of the stage. Tall waves are again beating against the platform-stage. The table vanishes, covered by wings. In the shimmer of stroboscopic lights, against the background of a large, billowing canvas, the black she-bat castigates Alonso and the two sinners for crimes committed and predicts their doom.

But although Prospero praises Ariel for his recitation, the prediction is drowned by loud thunder. In this spectacular show, Strehler again departed from the classical images of the baroque theater, where Virgilian myths, antique icons, and the symbolic banquet reappeared. The wonders and the awe of that theater were both antique and Christian. Shakespeare's Harpia utters a Virgilian prophecy from the *Aeneid*. The table with food and drink is a Renaissance banquet as well as a Last Supper from which the sinners were banished. It should have pitchers with water and wine and large loaves of bread on it. Shakespeare's usurpers go through the torture of hunger and thirst on the desert island.

The three men of sin give up their splendid garments as they escape in panic. Alonso will lose his crown. Ariel will pick up these Milanese riches and put them in the prop-room inside the island-platform. He will take them back when Caliban and the two drunken jesters return to carry out their attempt on Prospero's life. Pulcinella-Trinculo will throw the royal robe over his shoulders. Capitano-Stephano will put on the crown. Strehler wanted to repeat in buffo the symbols of usurpation and regicide. But in Shakespeare's histories, or even his comedies, a royal crown has never rested on the head of a clown. In the Shakespearean scenario, only glistening rags were hung out on the line by Ariel. When the water-drenched drunkards throw themselves on these, Caliban understands he is dealing with fools. He knows that Prospero's power is in the Book. But the book of Prospero is the director's script. For Strehler the operatic score is more important than a royal crown.

Strehler's Prospero does not want to part from his conductor's stick. In Shakespeare's *Tempest* Prospero drowns the book in the depths of the sea and breaks his staff in half after uttering Medea's terrible vows, as a prelude to the final scene of mercy. In the Milan *Tempest*, Prospero breaks his conductor's stick in half and tosses his operatic score into the orchestra pit at the very end of the drama.

Ariel's last service is to bring Prospero the insignia of the Duke of Milan, hidden away on the island during twelve years: a coat, a hat, and a rapier. In the *Tempest* of my imagination, the only thing left of the last dukedom is rags, eaten away by the seawater, while the rapier is brown with rust. In these rags the real Duke of Milan should stand before the usurpers wearing a cloth of gold and ermine, untouched by the ocean waves. Strehler's solutions are traditional, but, as in his entire interpretation and treatment of act 5, it is not a return to the Renaissance rigors or even to the baroque vision, but to a melodramatic, tame, and shallow nineteenth-century Shakespeare.

In this four-hour play, Strehler omitted the most cruel scene of the entire drama, where the actors playing Roman goddesses in a vision of the Golden Age and Lost Paradise turn into terrible shades of hunting dogs. At the finale of Strehler's *Tempest*, the buffoon Trinculo will sit at the feet of the King of Naples, while the repentant Caliban, watched by all the scoundrels who had been pardoned in the "brave new world," will return to his dark cave in the island.

Shakespeare's *Tempest* reverts to its beginning, so that everything can begin once more. It is a return to the time twelve years before the overture of the play, when Prospero, the Lord's anointed, was exiled from his dukedom and landed on a desert island where the rightful ruler, the Lord's non-anointed, was Caliban. Of all the possible endings in *The Tempest*, Caliban's return to his rock-prison seems the most false and revolting. When Prospero and the newcomers from the Old World leave the island, Caliban should remain alone on the stage: deceived twice, he is richer in experience only.

In the last scene of the play, before the epilogue, Prospero frees Ariel from the wire-chain, but he is not departing to the cold freedom far away from the world of mortals. The free Ariel crosses over the ramp and walks among the audience. When in the epilogue Prospero steps downstage, Ariel returns to sit at his feet. In the profound reading of *The Tempest*, life and theater, two spectacles and two illusions, send back their reflections, like two mirrors. The opposition of theater and life was replaced by Strehler with the unity of the stage and the audience. Shakespeare's Prospero in the epilogue walks down to the audience not only to ask for the applause but to pray for absolution, mercy, and release from the theater. He returns not to the people, not to the audience, but—to the seclusion of Milan—where one-third of his thoughts shall be devoted to death. Strehler's Prospero returns to a Milan which is the house of illusion and glory.

This surprising, disturbing, yet touching identification of the director with the character of the drama, of Strehler with Prospero, is the source of all the revelations and enchantments of the Milan *Tempest*, as well as all its limitations. Shakespeare's Prospero knows that when he dims the lights the actors will vanish into thin air like spirits and the Paradise Regained will change into a wooden platform, but Prospero-Strehler also knows that when he puts the lights on, the wooden platform will be transformed again into the golden sand from which Miranda and Ferdinand shall gaze at the rising sun.

These two theatrical visions have two different messages: the reduction of the golden age to an empty platform lays bare the illusion of the theater and the illusion of the myth; the transformation of the wooden platform into a Paradise Lost is an affirmation of the theater, which recreates myths. Prospero-Strehler breaks his magic wand and throws it to the bottom of the sea, knowing that in an instant the stage manager in the orchestra pit will hand him a new conductor's stick. The Milan version of *The Tempest*, despite all its beauty, has almost nothing of the Shakespearean bitterness and renunciation.

Translated by Barbara Krzywicka

Note
Strehler's *Tempest* was performed for the first time in Milan on June 28, 1978. Since that first performance Strehler has modified his staging at least twice. In the last version, at the ending, the whole structure collapsed into a spectacular nothingness and from this nothingness once again emerged the stage. In Strehler's world and ethos, the stage could perish only for a short instant.

Ran, or The End of the World

Madness awaits everyone at the close of that cold night. "These four are already mad," wrote Camus about *King Lear*, "one is mad by profession, another by choice, and two from the suffering they could not bear." The jester is the madman by profession; Edgar, in order to save his life; Lear escapes into madness; and Kent alone tries to fend it off to the very last. The scene in which the three exiles find their last refuge from a raging Nature in the abject hut where Edgar had hidden himself earlier is the key scene for every interpretation of *Lear*, but even more so for a theatrical or cinematic vision of the play.

In both the theatrical and film versions of Peter Brook's *King Lear*, a Beckettian dialogue between human cripples takes place on the sack bedding in the mud hut, and it is here that the madmen judge Goneril and Regan, personified by two overturned wooden stools.

In Grigori Kozintsev's film adaptation of *King Lear*, almost twenty years ago, the abandoned hovel, where the exiled old man who was once king finds his last shelter, teems with human bodies. Old men and women, cripples shaking their stubby limbs, women nursing infants and even a *yurodivy* ("God's fool"), intoning unending litanies which mix with "poor Tom's" exorcisms, sit everywhere—on rags, sacks, or the bare ground—and fill every corner, every wall, packed, one on top of another. In Kozintsev's dramaturgy, the exiles from the royal court pass "refugees" streaming into the steppe from razed settlements and villages. In that enormous shack, the mad ruler and his subjects find themselves sharing a common Russian fate: poverty, degradation, and suffering.

In Kurosawa's *King Lear*, it appears, for just an instant, that there is no one in the abandoned hut which the former ruler, jester, and his last servant have finally reached. But a strange figure glimmers in the darkness. By the feeble light of a candle stub, the newcomers can make out hair falling over someone's eyes. The figure turns out to be a blind man. Hidetora, the Japanese Lear, recognizes the blind man as one whose life he did not take, but whose eyes he had put out. The blind man was allowed to keep only a flute, given to him by his sister, and it is on this flute that he now plays to Hidetora. Just as in those scenes in the Kabuki where the murderer returns to the scene of the crime, the flute wails over the orchestra, moans, rises in more and more penetrating tones, as if it were tearing not only at the ears but at the heart as well. The memory and reproach of the flute is unbearable. The Japanese Lear, exiled by the voice of the flute, flees the cottage and submits himself again to the storm and torrential rains. "This tempest will not give me leave to ponder/On things would hurt me more."

In even the most illusionistic scenography, the decorations in the theater are always conventional. In the film, the landscape is real. Of all the royal tragedies, *King Lear* probably most needs a real landscape. Yet the selection of landscape in *Lear* is, perhaps more than in any other play, simultaneously a selection of costume and historical time. In *King Lear*, the question "where?" is also the question "when?" Bakhtin's chronotope, his unit of time-place, has a different degree of reality in film than in theater. In Shakespeare's dramas, the other place, the other "historicity," is, at the same time, the plays' other universality. And what is more, the other place is often their other contemporaneity.

Everyone, adapters as well as stage producers, has had to grapple with the historical setting of *King Lear*. The play has been transported to the time of Druids with menhirs built on stage. There was even a production where Lear was ruler of the Aztecs. Peter Brook wanted to avoid a narrow historicity in both of his productions, the stage adaptation at Stratford in 1967 and the film version five years later. He situated his Lear somewhere in the epoch of William the Conqueror, but at the same time he veered from all historical verisimilitude. He dressed his actors in the simplest costumes: furs, boots, and long, voluminous robes. He wanted to suggest the severity and primacy of the Renaissance court while at the same time showing its sophistication and menace. Brook transported the film version into the cold landscape of Jutland. Kozintsev took his *Lear* into the Russian steppe—a Russian Orthodox priest presided at the wedding of the King of France and Cordelia.

Brook's Jutland and Kozintsev's broad Russian steppe were a way of introducing *Lear* into universal history. Kurosawa took a drama of *Lear* into medieval Japan. For the second time since *Throne of Blood*, his striking adaptation of *Macbeth*, Kurosawa has discovered another historical place for Shakespeare's royal dramas. In the period before the consolidation of the almost absolute power of the shogun, samurai clans, whose power depended on mercenary armies and the blind obedience of their vassals, ravaged the land and killed one another. There are striking analogies between these wars and the Wars of the Roses in England, or perhaps even more between these samurai wars and the fratricidal battles and unceasing betrayals of Scottish clans.

In Kurosawa's *Ran*, Hidetora, lord of a wooden fortress, has extended his rule to the limits of the horizon—all three castles situated on distant hills and visible from the camp tent now belong to him. In the twilight of his years, the cruel tyrant divides his kingdom, among sons, however, not daughters.

Kurosawa's greatness lies in his capacity to reveal historical similarity and variance, to find a Shakespearean sense of doom in the other, remote and apparently alien historical place. He trims the plot to the bone. Hidetora's three sons are all that remains of Lear's three daughters and Gloucester's two sons. Shakespeare had doubled the plot of the old folk tale about three daughters (two vile and one noble): Kurosawa has cut and compressed it. In this Japanese condensation of plot and character, only the eldest son's wife, a

remnant from Goneril and Regan, is left in the castle where
Hidetora has murdered her entire family. In this samurai
epic, it is her drive for vengeance that destroys Hidetora's
clan and legacy.

In the first scene of *Ran*, the aged Hidetora dozes off
before his tent in the noonday sun. His youngest son fells
three small trees and plants them next to his sleeping father
to provide him with shade. This is how Cordelia's mute de-
votion is translated into the signs of another theater. In *Ran*,
the Goneril/Regan in one body grows to the dimensions of
a new forbidding Lady Macbeth, but her immobile, glassy,
and white face with uplifted brows is like the mask of the
woman-vampire and woman-serpent in the Noh theater. In
the movie's only love scene, she commits violence before she
yields. Seizing a sword, she slashes at the neck of Hidetora's
second-born, who has murdered her husband, the eldest of
the sons. Now this second son will become the instrument of
her revenge. The long, white sash of her kimono falls to the
empty mat and slowly unwinds like a serpent. In the Kabuki
theater and in the custom which is still honored, the sash of
the kimono thrown to the floor is a sign of sexual compliance.
The vengeful sister-in-law in *Ran* demands the head of her
lover's wife. A standard prop in Elizabethan theater was a
head in a small cage. Similarly, in the Kabuki a standard prop
is a head wrapped in rags. In Kurosawa's version of *Lear*, the
Goneril/Regan character unwraps just such a head. But it is
not the head of her lover's wife, but the sculpted, stone head
of a fox.

In an early scene in Laurence Olivier's film version of
Richard the Third, pages are carrying crowns, set on vermillion
pillows, into the Coronation Hall. They trip on the stairs and
the crowns, destined for the royal brothers, fall to the scarlet
carpet. Twenty-five years have gone by and I remember only
that one scene from the entire film. It has settled into my
memory like Shakespeare's aphorisms, which are the essence
of the drama. In the language of film, that short scene with
the falling crowns is also its essence. In Kozintsev's *Hamlet*,
which has also become history, Ophelia is put into a rigid
corset before she is led into the royal chambers. In Rome a

few years ago I attended a large exhibit of instruments of torture spanning the time from the Middle Ages to our own century. I saw steel cages with spikes inside that were designed to dig into the flesh. Except for the spikes, Ophelia's corset was similar to that instrument of torture.

In the last scene of Kurosawa's *Throne of Blood*, Macbeth hangs from the walls bristling with arrows like an enormous dying porcupine. The farther that other time-place in Shakespeare's dramas is from Elizabethan England, the less likely it is that the image will match the text. It stops being an illustration and becomes its essence and sign. In *Throne of Blood* and *Ran*, Shakespeare is moved not just into another cultural circle but into another theater. And herein lies Kurosawa's genius and the singularity of his Shakespeare. The theater is Noh and Kabuki.

Noh is medieval theater and Kabuki would be considered late Renaissance theater by our standards of periodization. But it is exactly here that we find amazing chronological surprises: the years around 1600, when *Hamlet* was first performed, mark the beginning of Kabuki theater. But it is not chronology that is the most important. Of the two extreme choices at the disposal of a modern producer of Shakespeare's royal tragedies—that is, historicism and anachronism—faithfulness to history (but which history!) seems the most deceptive. The costume, of course, can be faithfully copied from a museum, but an actor—who is unfamiliar with the gestures of the ruler or the heir awaiting the falling crown—must know how to move in the trappings of another age. Even when the scene takes place in the bedchamber of the queen or concubine, the modern actor knows only the rudimentary gestures of sex. Perhaps this is why modern film adaptations of *Macbeth* prefer to show Lady Macbeth in the nude.

It seems that the traditions of Japanese feudal culture have endured. The rituals of the conjugal bath, arrangement of flowers, and tea ceremony are still rigidly observed. Of course they may simply be gestures and empty signs, but gestures and signs are the basic matter of theater. Classic Japanese theater has preserved them, lent them an enduring form, and repeats them unchanged. The wife of Hidetora's eldest son and the concubine of his second-born bites at the hem of her kimono in an attack of furious weeping, just as the Bunraku dolls and geishas in Kabuki cry and bite the hems of their kimonos in fits of jealousy. But the Japanese theater has not only preserved the gestures and signs of amorous passion in family dramas, it has also preserved the court ceremonies, receiving of vassals, dispatching of envoys with secret letters, acts of allegiance and betrayal, and the battles of entire armies as pageant and action, just as in Shakespeare's royal tragedies. On the stage of the Kabuki, two great samurai armies, cavalry and infantry, are represented by four, maybe eight, warriors. They wear the same leather helmets and move in the same easy steps, they draw their bows and shoot with a simultaneous gesture. The two armies differ only in the color of the large streamers attached like wings to their shoulders.

In Kurosawa's long, almost three-hour film epic, it seems that almost one-third of the film is devoted to battle scenes. Thousands of people appear to be taking part in them. The cavalry rushes to the attack at a more and more frenzied pace. The infantry moves with the same rocking, oblivious rush. From the opposite side the cavalry breaks into a trot, then into a gallop, spears lowered. The infantry runs in the same thrust of bodies. Red and blue, then white and black.

Lear's three daughters are replaced by Hidetora's three sons. The theme is fratricidal war. The castle gates are rammed open. The reds pour in like rivers of ants, while the blues pour out in another stream. Nothing but arrow-studded bodies remains on the ramparts and turrets of the castle, nothing but bodies are left speared to the floor. Kurosawa is the distinct and peerless master of battle scenes. Even the cruelest of them makes you gasp in amazement. They are a vision of the Apocalypse rendered with the highest artistic perfection.

The enormous castle constructed of wooden beams which Hidetora assailed and conquered years ago, the castle in which he murdered every last man, is now set afire. Hidetora remains in it alone. His guards have all been shot or speared. The bodies of concubines, who ran themselves through with daggers, litter the floor of the neighboring room. The flames approach the throne where Hidetora sits. He runs to the roof of the fortress where he sees the fields covered with his son's armies. Hidetora runs down into the courtyard. The soldiers step aside for the old man who runs like a ghost out of the flames. The son takes out his sword. But neither he nor his generals has the heart to kill the old man. Hidetora steps out through the gates of the fortress into the green fields. His last journey leads him through these green hills and fields. The faithful exile and the jester, the two nurses of the madman, will serve him until his death. The jester puts a crown of reeds on his head. Hidetora crawls through the rushes like a large child, in white clothes, on all fours, picking flowers. The two armies, the red and the black, occupy their starting positions on opposing hillsides.

From then on, everything happens as in Shakespeare. Except that the youngest of his sons, not Cordelia, finds Hidetora. But briefly. The youngest son dies in an ambush arranged by his older brother. And, as in Shakespeare, the Japanese Lear dies holding the expiring body in his arms. "As flies to wanton boys are we to the gods. They kill us for their sport." The lines uttered by Gloucester at the height of his experience are spoken by Kurosawa's jester.

A few years ago, during a break from sessions at one of the Shakespeare conferences, I asked two of my colleagues, over a whiskey on the rocks, for the day was hot, "Who succeeds Lear?" "The Duke of Albany is still one of the titles of English kings," said the first colleague, "and it is clear to every civilized Briton that Goneril's husband, the Duke of Albany, would inherit the throne after Lear." "Even my grad students," said the Italian professor, "who have just nicked Aristotle, think it is obvious that noble Edgar must succeed Lear in keeping with the logic of a tragedy." "Every Pole," I said, "in keeping with his personal and historical experience, is certain that no one will succeed Lear. The world in which Lear lived has been rent asunder and it will never grow back together again."

Ran means "fury, chaos, madness" in Japanese. In the last scene, the blind man feels his way along the threshold of the gutted castle to the edge of a precipice. Fleeing the assassins, he left his flute behind. His sister returned for the flute and left him a roll of parchment with a picture of the Buddha. Kurosawa understood that in the architectonics of *Lear*, even in the most remote adaptation, Cordelia's place could not remain completely vacant. The eyes of this Buddhist Cordelia's brother were put out. Hidetora ordered the rest of her family murdered. Later Hidetora married her off to his middle son. She alone does not hate. But perhaps in the broader perspective of nothing at all, pity and hate come alike to naught.

But not even she is left alive. Her head is cut off when she returns for the flute. The wife of the eldest son, who had asked for the head, is also dead. Hidetora is dead, as are all his sons. The blind man feels his way to the edge of the abyss. The parchment falls from his hands and unrolls over the bluff where the wind gently rocks the likeness of the smiling Buddha. The sky is light blue, streaked with gentle, slow-moving clouds. The blue sky is completely empty.

This is also the color of the winter sky in Santa Monica, California, where I now live. Some miles southeast of Santa Monica, in Irvine, the sky is perhaps even bluer. Coral trees bloom bright red and give off a strong fragrance even in February. The Irvine campus is one of the most extensive in the United States. It seems to be empty, because of an enormous garden, almost a forest. The campus stretches imperceptibly into the desert. There at the edge of the campus, Jerzy Grotowski has a wooden shack that houses the last of his theater-laboratories. The shack is empty, furnished only with a torn drum. Next to the shack Grotowski has built a Siberian yurt out of light, still fragrant wood. The floor of the yurt is waxed, and those entering it remove their shoes. There is no furniture except for a crude table that stands against one wall.

Grotowski's "Poor Theater" has not existed for years. Three of the actors have died, all the others—actors, co-workers, and students—are scattered all over the world. Behind the yurt stretches a green meadow, where horses graze as in a painting by Gauguin. Beyond that is stark desert. At night, coyotes come as close as Grotowski's yurt. At noon, when the sun is the hottest, you can hear the clattering whir of rattlesnakes.

Translated by Lillian Vallee

The Cruel Webster

For Zbigniew Raszewski

In the first scene of act 1 of *The White Devil*, in exactly the tenth second of the dialogue, the words "Fortune's a right whore" resound in the house. Seldom before had such a brutal and violent condemnation of Fortune rung from the English stage. In Greco-Roman tradition the wheel of fortune pictured the changeable and unpredictable varieties of human fate. Although Fortune was usually represented with a blindfold over her eyes, she was not entirely "blind." She cautioned the mighty and proud of this world against the envy of the gods and a careless confidence in their own powers. In the Middle Ages, the changeable wheel of fortune became the outward image of the fate of rulers. In *The Holkham Bible Picture Book*, from the early fourteenth century, one of the most beautiful English manuscripts, the wheel of Fortune bears four views of a monarch. In the first he is a youth with streaming hair and a crown raised in one hand as he rises to the top of this ferris wheel of royal fate: *Regnabo*. At the very top the still youthful ruler is shown with crown and sceptre: *Regno*. He ages quickly, however. When next we see him, his beard is gray, his hair matted, and he tumbles headlong from the same wheel, scattering both crown and sceptre: *Regnavi*. Finally, at the very bottom, deprived of royal ornament and insignia, he lies shriveled and barefoot in a threadbare cloak: *Sum sine regno*.

In act 3 of *The Duchess of Malfi*, Webster again calls on the image of the wheel of fortune: "When Fortune's wheel is

overcharg'd with princes,/The weight makes it move swift."
The heavier its weight, the swifter the wheel. Webster's apho-
rism is most striking—even though it is repeated from an
earlier tragedy—for its use of princes in the plural. In Shakespeare's histories, rulers are raised by, then fall from this
medieval wheel of fortune. The Anointed King punishes the
great feudal princes for their disobedience and rebellion. He
wages wars and imposes new taxes. He once was adored and
now is hated. His Usurper, waiting at the foot of the wheel,
promises a just governance and the rectification of all wrongs.
The citizens of London throw their caps into the air at the
sight of him, the magnates plot with him. However, to assume
the throne he must murder first his enemies, and later his
headstrong allies, so that when he finally dons the crown, he
will be as hated as the ruler he replaces. In the meantime,
the son or nephew of the murdered or exiled ruler awaits
the next turn of the Great Mechanism.

In the same first scene of act 1 in *The White Devil*, early
in the tragedy, after no longer than two or three minutes of
action, the workings of fortune are recalled in another image:
"This well goes well with two buckets: I must tend/The pouring out of either." One always rises, the other sinks as the
wheel turns. The wheel of fortune was not only a likely model
for Shakespeare's histories, but also the most common and
characteristic element of the tragedy of revenge during the
Elizabethan and Jacobean periods. In these tragedies, conceived as imitations of Seneca, there are also two antagonists:
the Villain and the Avenger. Revenge must first entail discovery of the crime and then be made equal to the original
transgression in cruelty. If revenge were dealt to the guilty
immediately, the drama would be over in the first scene. The
Avenger thinks through the means of revenge and prepares
it slowly, systematically, in cold blood, with a complete and
calculated cruelty. When he finds himself at the height of the
wheel of fortune, his hands will be spattered with as much
blood as stains the hands of the murderer on whom he wreaks
his vengeance. And both, one after the other, will come crash-
ing to the bottom. In this model of tragedy, the Anointed
King and the Usurper, the Villain and the Avenger, are lev-
eled by one and the same fate.

"When the bad bleeds, then is the tragedy good," says the protagonist of Tourneur's *The Revenger's Tragedy*, which precedes *The White Devil* by five years. And again, near the play's epilogue, "No power is angry when the lustful die;/When thunder claps, heaven likes the tragedy." But not just the guilty shed their blood in the tragedy of revenge—everybody dies together, the guilty and the innocent. If *Titus Andronicus* had a sixth act, the first two rows of spectators would be next to be slaughtered because none of the principal dramatis personae remains alive at the end of the fifth.

Titus Andronicus is one of Shakespeare's earliest plays, yet one cannot say that the death toll in his mature masterpiece, *Hamlet*, decreases. In that play's epilogue, even before Hamlet dies, three corpses already litter the stage: those of Laertes, the king and the queen. Earlier, Polonius is mistakenly but effectively stabbed through a curtain. Ophelia throws herself into the brook, and Hamlet sends Rosencrantz and Guildenstern to their beheading in England—not to mention the number of soldiers and natives killed in the war by Fortinbras "to gain a little patch of ground" in the ever devastated Poland.

The wheel of fortune, which in the Middle Ages and early Renaissance denoted the mercilessness and severity, but also to some degree the universal justice of fate, has become a wheel of torture by the close of the Renaissance. "I am bound/ Upon a wheel of fire," says Lear on the verge of madness. "For my part,/The rack, the gallows, and the torturing wheel,/ Shall be sound sleeps to me," says the avenger in *The White Devil* an instant before his death. Ultimately, the wheel of fortune becomes the equal of the gallows or the executioner's hammer. It becomes nothing but a means of destroying the condemned. Blind Fortune will open her eyes just once more in Webster. "And Fortune seems only to have her eyesight/ To behold my tragedy," cries the Duchess of Malfi from her dungeon.

"As flies to wanton boys are we to the gods./They kill us for their sport," says the blinded Gloucester at the beginning of his final wandering. "We are merely the stars' tennis-balls, struck and bandied/Which way please them," says Bosola in *The Duchess of Malfi* when by mistake in the dark he kills the very man he wants to save. Webster has exchanged the gods, who kill us as flies, for the stars, which play tennis with us. Tennis was a favored entertainment at Renaissance courts, though it was played according to different rules than those used currently. In *The White Devil*, the Duke of Brachiano, the lover of the treacherous Vittoria, changes his shirt in her room after returning from a round of tennis. The tragedy and comedy of manners, always bitter and venomous, are differently mixed in Webster than in Shakespeare.

> VITTORIA: Do you mean to die indeed?
> FLAMINEO: With as much pleasure
>   As e'er my father gat me.

This is almost the last conversation between Vittoria and her brother, her murderer and her bawd. Webster was undoubtedly the most persistent successor to the dark Shakespeare. Yet often this is the Shakespeare of *Hamlet* and *Lear* mixed strangely with the Shakespeare of *Measure for Measure*, this mongrel of scoffing tragedy with a sarcastic comedy. "O me! this place is hell," shouts Vittoria, when she finds the poisoned and strangled body of her lover. "This place is hell," but in Webster hell is primarily on stage. The horror for Shakespeare is the essence of the real world. In Webster the aim of the horrifying scenes is, like Hitchcock's in our time, to terrify and to shock the viewers.

In *The White Devil*, the first two murders are shown only in dumb-show. In contemporary terms taken from film and television, we would say that they are visuals without sound. Brachiano summons a wizard to his room at night to conjure the scenes of the murders before his eyes. He sees his unhappy wife kneel at the side of their nuptial bed and pray, then, before going to sleep, kiss her husband's portrait. The painting has been poisoned and she falls to the ground lifeless. Immediately after this comes the next dumb-show: the unhappy cuckold, husband to the deceiving Vittoria, jumps over a vaulting horse for morning exercise. Brachiano's henchman throws him to the ground and "writhes his neck about."

The Duchess of Malfi is subjected to the most extravagant moral tortures. She is given the sundered hand of a corpse and led to believe that she is clasping the hand of her husband. She sees "behind a traverse, the artificial figures of Antonio and his children, appearing as if they were dead."

> These presentations are but framed in wax
> By the curious master in that quality,
> Vincentio Laurola, and she takes them
> For true substantial bodies.

After Marlowe and Shakespeare, when the tragic themes are exhausted, post-Elizabethan theater attempts to arouse the jaded sensibility of the spectator by increasingly violent means. Webster is not only a continuator of the dark Shakespeare, he is also a precursor of new dramatic genres and a new theatrical style. When theaters reopened their doors after Cromwell's revolution, the melodrama became the leading show. The rejected wife praying at the empty nuptial bed was one of the most typical scenes of the *comedie larmoyante*, the lachrymose bourgeois comedy, and of the melodrama which triumphed on the English and, soon after, the French stage.

Wax figures spurting blood or severed members bathed in red stage lighting forecast the theater of horrors which has survived to our day in the French Grand Guignol and in Anglo-American thrillers. Poisoned helmets, Bibles, and portraits all belong to this theater, a theater in which the spectators are treated to the groans of madmen coming from offstage, to screams and cries and dismal moans. "How miserable a thing is to die/'Mongst women howling!" This theater also has a penchant for frequent ghosts and a multiplicity of hauntings.

Of course, there are also ghosts in Shakespeare: the ghost of Hamlet's father, Banquo's ghost in *Macbeth*, and the ghosts of the murdered in *Richard III*. But these are awe-inspiring ghosts, "real" ghosts. They reveal crimes, exhort survivors to revenge, predict defeat. There can be no tragedy without such ghosts. Not only must the protagonists believe in their appearance, or at least in the dramatic sense of their message, but so must the viewers. Webster's ghosts are a mere illusion: ". . . how strong Imagination works! how she can frame/Things which are not! . . . Did ever/Man dream awake till now? Remove this object:/Out of my brain with't . . ." More theatrical than the ghost of the poisoned Isabelle in *The White Devil* is the ghost of Brachiano, who like a second-rate Hamlet holds "a pot of lily-flowers, with a skull in it."

Besides being a forerunner of the horror theater and the bourgeois melodrama, Webster is also the difficult, and astounding precursor of yet another theater, another sensibility, and another aesthetic, for which it is not easy to find the appropriate term. One could call it an aesthetic and sensibility that are at the same time romantic and modernist. "Will you turn your body, / Which is the goodly palace of the soul, / To the soul's slaughter house?" This is an astonishing and hallucinatory image—the slaughter house of the soul. It does not seem to belong to a seventeenth-century vocabulary. It sounds like a progeny of Kierkegaard, or even more like a superb unknown quote from Artaud's Manifesto of the Theater of Cruelty.

In *The White Devil*, Duke Francesco ends his great monologue, in which he plots the black design of his revenge, with an unexpected quote from the *Aeneid*: "*Flectere si nequeo superos, Acheronta movebo.*" Freud affixed this same quote (about moving the dark forces of the underground when the power of the heavens will not help) as the epigraph to *The Interpretation of Dreams*, in the year 1899. This is an interesting coincidence, but perhaps not as surprising as it at first appears. "I account this world a tedious theatre/For I do play a part in 't 'gainst my will," says the Duchess of Malfi when cast into the dungeon. ". . . A good actor many times is curs'd/For playing a villain part," says Ferdinand to his henchman. Only Julia, a woman "of pleasure," does not know "uncertain wishes and unquiet longings." All the main characters of both Webster tragedies, not just his two great heroines, but also his *bravi*, avengers, and *condottieri* of crime, are partially sunk in darkness. It is as if they were poorly cast actors with ill-matched roles or playing more than one role simultaneously.

Vittoria Corombona, "the famous Venetian Curtizan," is shameless in her first scene. She is ready to sleep with the Duke of Brachiano in her marital bedroom, even in the presence of her own mother, as soon as the doors shut behind her husband. And she immediately plots to dispose of that husband and her lover's wife. Her brother, her mother, even her lover call her a whore and strumpet over and over again. In the court scene, however, she suddenly changes into a great lady unjustly accused of complicity in murder and adultery. She acts magnificently. She not only convinces the ambassadors attending the trial of her innocence, she not only convinces us, the audience, but she manages to convince even herself. "Ha! whore! what's that!" She comes to believe in her own innocence. Webster is a master at showing the various costumes in the wardrobe of the soul. He is an even greater master of death scenes. Vittoria dies like a great tragic heroine. She dies theatrically but grandly. "O, my greatest sin lay in my blood!/Now my blood pays for 't."

The torture and death of the Duchess of Malfi is accompanied by dancing, giggling, and the obscene name-calling of the madmen led to the door of her cell. She dies in the trappings of a bad horror theater. Before she dies, however, she utters two lines devastating in their simplicity. "I am Duchess of Malfi still," and later, when her executioners have appeared with the rope, she says to her nurse Cariola: "I pray thee, look thou giv'st my little boy/Some syrup for his cold, and let the girl/Say her prayers ere she sleep." Webster is merciless: Cariola is also strangled.

There is more darkness in *The Duchess of Malfi* than in *The White Devil*. Ferdinand, the Duke of Calabria, brother to the Duchess, swears that he never wants to see her face. And the candles are snuffed when he enters her bedchamber. The darkness in *The Duchess of Malfi* is not just dramatic, it is also symbolic. The brothers wreak vengeance on their sister, because, as a widow, she remarried her own steward against their will. But wounded family pride does not justify the torture inflicted on the Duchess. Ferdinand covers her with vile names in the first scene, as if he wanted to tear the clothes from her body. He destroys his twin sister, his likeness, as if he wanted to punish himself for desiring her. He stifles the black libido in himself.

The word "incest" does not appear once in this tragedy. The motives are transposed and hidden. This incongruity of the conscious and the concealed is Webster's great dramatic achievement and psychological discovery. The brother imprisons his twin sister in a dark cave, but he himself never leaves his own darkness. He believes he is a werewolf and goes mad. "Give me some wet hay, I am broken-winded-/I do account this world but a dog-kennel."

Ferdinand lacks self-knowledge, but Flamineo and Bosola, the henchmen of their respective masters and the executors of their crimes, have an excess of self-awareness. They procure for their masters, they murder and spy (Webster still uses the old word for a spy and informer: "intelligencer," which has survived, of course, in Intelligence Service). They have no choice, there is no vile thing that they are unprepared to do. For themselves they reserve just one privilege: to have no illusions. They know everything about themselves, everything about their masters, and almost everything about the world in which they live. And they die with complete self-awareness. As Flamineo says in *The White Devil* when asked by his murderer what he is thinking of on the brink of death:

> Nothing; of nothing: leave thy idle question.
> I am i' the way to study a long silence:
> To prate were idle. I remember nothing.
> There's nothing of so infinite vexation
> As man's own thoughts.

Macbeth saw the same nothingness when he departed for darkness:

> Life's but a walking shadow; a poor player,
> That struts and frets his hour upon the stage,
> And then is heard no more: it is a tale
> Told by an idiot, full of sound and fury,
> Signifying nothing.

In Flamineo's last monologue, the cruel Webster equals the cruel Shakespeare.

Translated by Lillian Vallee

Index